Alongside We Travel

Contemporary Poets on Autism

Alongside We Travel

Contemporary Poets on Autism

Edited by

Sean Thomas Dougherty

The New York Quarterly Foundation, Inc.
New York, New York

NYQ Books™ is an imprint of The New York Quarterly Foundation, Inc.

The New York Quarterly Foundation, Inc.
P. O. Box 2015
Old Chelsea Station
New York, NY 10113

www.nyq.org

First Edition

Set in New Baskerville

Layout by Raymond P. Hammond

On the Cover:

Library of Congress Control Number:

ISBN: 978-1-63045-058-8

Alongside We Travel

Contemporary Poets on Autism

Contents

Introduction

The Grace of the Aggrieved: Poetry and Autism

There is a common saying in autism communities, "I might not know everything about autism, but I know my autistic child." The diversity of this disability can run from the idiot-savant-Rain-Man ideal often perpetuated through popular culture, to a child being simply "quirky" or "prone to outbursts," to a really devastating physical and intellectual disability that can be devastating for a family. When I began to publicly propose this anthology, I had a well-known disability critic say to me, and I will quote him exactly "This is wonderful news. But please don't publish too many poems by whining aggrieved parents. I say this as a parent of a young man with autism. A young man whom I cherish exactly as he is." His response though a fine sentiment is also rather useless. What if your child must live with a profound disability that causes him or her pain, and as a parent you must witness this for a life? This critic's response gets to the core reason why I wanted to publish an anthology on autism. I wanted to hear the poems of those aggrieved parents alongside the ones who profess to have no regrets. I wanted to hear the voices of caregivers and cousins, witnesses and the guilty. I wanted to hear, if accomplished, the voices of autistic artists. What this critic failed to understand both as a parent and as an artist, was the ability to empathize and feel compassion outside of his own experience.

That is the job of poetry.

In this anthology you will find poems of love and friendship, of sorrow and loss and hope told from a variety of perspectives. There are pieces on autism from tutors and teachers, aunts and grandmothers, friends and siblings, and even from poets with autism themselves. Many of the poems though are from poet-parents of autistic children. These poems cover a lifetime of work, from young fathers to poet-mothers who have raised and written about their children well into adulthood, poems that span decades. I need to warn you. Many poems here are brutally honest, and show not just love but the frustrations, guilts, angers, and disappointments that arise from engagement with a disability that may cause chaos and despair, as well as evoke love. This anthology shows the true unflinching range of experience for writers involved in the disability of autism. This is a book by artists, making art out of the struggles of their lives.

Here you will find a variety of forms and approaches as you turn the pages: a textured crown of sonnets, tercets and couplets, poems in traditional stanzas and balanced shapes, prose-poems, story poems, and lyrics. Some poets confront and appropriate the institutional language and documents of autism to create new experimental poetic forms. These poets reimagine those often-dehumanizing documents and reclaim them to portray and explore the humanness of their son or daughter or friend in the face of the bureaucratic languages of Otherness. The diversity of approach reflects the diversity of experience the autism spectrum encompasses.

This anthology highlights the commonalities of experience across borders gathering writers from Canada, the United States, the UK and Israel. I can only hope these poems do for you, the reader, what they have taught me, the editor, about my own autistic daughter, about art, and how we can be brought together through language towards love. This is a book that can teach us about hope even while feeling aggrieved or betrayed by the world. A book to sing those we care for and who teach us every day about the diversity of what it means to be a human being.

Sean Thomas Dougherty
Erie Pennsylvania

Alongside We Travel

Contemporary Poets on Autism

Meredith Bergmann

Nursery Rhyme

Some years a single sentence comes—a freak—
but I saved everything you ever said
from those few early years when you could speak.
Beneath each crystal lens they can be read
and understood. I was a careful clerk.
I am the reliquary of your words.
They would make statues weep, but cannot work
the necessary miracle. Unheard,
unvoiced, untasted, charming phrases fade;
but copied out like prayers they gain the voice,
the lilt of poetry. And weren't they made
in flashes of imaginative choice?
One snowy afternoon when talk was cheap,
you said to me, "It's raining cats and sheep."

Tautavel Man

I

We drive into the valley from sharp crags
and follow its gentle tilt to Tautavel.
The map is no help. Unseen, but embarrassed,
unable to find the stair from the gorge,
unwilling to accept the incongruous door
set high in the cliff, we hunt for signs.
You sleep in the car and leave us in confusion.

By turns, your weary father and I at noon
climb, sweating, up the olive-covered slope
and find the cave, door open, cool and full
of students, charts, and picks. The dusty air
is occupied by intersecting strings.
Here Homo Sapiens, displacing bats,
flutters and gropes with tiny dental tools.
Each student seeks the elusive indications
that separate the diner from the dinner.
(Some centuries the cave belonged to bears.)

Before the gift of fire, art or burial
his silent skull was large enough for language.
He crouched here, honing hunting skills by watching
from the safety of the high cave's empty socket:
the steep-walled valley, the stealthy predator,
the panicked herd: driven, culled and eaten.
Year after year this lesson was repeated.
At my feet, fossil teeth gnaw through the dirt.
The students smoke and neck on the balcony.
Soon enough, perhaps, they will be parents.

You sleep in the car. Your father waits, unfed,
so I can visit the museum and grow lightheaded
wandering among exhibits from the cave.
Here, excavated meals are reassembled
and brandish fangs and claws, edible monsters.

Nearby, the family in a diorama
suck raw bloody bones, their heavy mouths
expressionless, intent upon their marrow.
And here *Homo erectus* sits before me
cast in plaster from a living child.
Despite his food, the boy's face is remarkably clean.

      II
Wake now, my son
that I may resume that study
from which there can be no vacation.
Day after day I scan
the beautiful plain of your face
across which frowns and smiles
march like trained elephants
or flee at a simple word.
Come, my cub, let us play.
The car is littered with animals
and brilliant plastic fish.
Every single one
is very deeply gnawed,
but none of them is named.
I cannot call them toys.

I hunger to know your mind.
Before the questions spark
before lies flicker and catch
before the tale of the beast and the castle
you surface for a moment, sharp
and bright among the ages
and your eyes look just like ours.

Lesson

with Soma Mukhopadhyay,
who has taught hundreds of autistic children
to communicate by pointing to letters
July, 2008

We learn that love and worry cannot cure.
There must be some dispassionate insistence,
some standard fixed
some distance
from which to see the slightest hint of turning.

A tiny woman in a tiny room,
she leads you, wailing, yet not quite rebelling,
to break your spell
by spelling.
She knows her love must be the love of learning.

You learn your self a letter at a time.
And all your teachers wish they'd been the one
and wonder what
she's done
that they have not, for all their love and yearning.

How can your breakthrough be that swift and sure?
What did you understand? What do you know?
We are left stunned
and slow
to learn to see beyond her first discerning.

The Ransom

When one has sold the dream boat and not wept,
the family jewelry, the island villa
(not unlike the places some are kept)
and prayed as if devout that they not kill the
loved one, stolen on a night all slept
too deep,

and after welcoming with singing heart
that lost one, home at last from basement, cave,
abandoned warehouse, truck or car or cart,
and seen him healed and realized one was brave
as he was, won't the jubilation start
to seep

away as one begins to miss some thing
(more easily idealized treasure), sold
and now beyond one's reach, will one not wring
the ransom out in guilt if not in gold
and wander in a darkness that can't bring
one sleep?

We tried for years to get you back, and twice
we lost you even more as you regressed.
We measure, now, each hour in a precise
negotiation of our worst and best,
because you've asked us not to make your price
too steep.

Catching the Eye

The Great Hunt, floor mosaic c. 350 AD, Villa Romana del Casale

I read bits of the guidebook to my son,
a young man, glancing down at the mosaic.
Perhaps the cruel story will distress him:
it's full of details of a Roman hunt
for wild beasts taken for the Coliseum.
He looks at art and sees his own condition,
predicament, and fate. He sees the cages,
the circus animals, the stinking ship,
and, lower, how to fool a mother tiger.
To steal her cubs away from Africa,
you bring a mirrored sphere from Rome and roll it
before the frantic beast, who grips it, thinking
her own reflection is her captured cub.
And then you ride away with all her young.

When little, he'd spend hours in front of glass.
He wasn't fascinated just by mirrors,
shop windows, or sleek surfaces like pools.
Sometimes it was the images beyond.
Sometimes he'd search my face, quite close to me,
and gaze into my eyes. Something was wrong
(we call it autism). He wasn't seeing
my seeing. I couldn't really catch his eye.
And even after I removed my glasses,
his ever-faithful mirrors, I saw that he
was making contact with his fleeting self
reflected on the surface of my eyes.
But he outgrew this. Has he seen enough?
He nods, across the hapless animals.

YVONNE BLOMER

Sonnet for a newborn now seven

Underground we were, below the citadel,
my son, newborn, asleep on my chest.
On the streets above, Italian flowed like mother's milk
in heat. We were in a cathedral or under it. We felt
the etched walls for markings—birds or other animals.
The monks, or a priest above, began to sing. Was it *Ave Maria*
that fell through stone, through the ages and knowledge of stone?
Sound, thrum in the chest, entered us. Out of the corner of my eye
or my imagination, I saw a boy leaning in, he was my son, now.
His hands are small, so perfect, though one pinky finger
a little crooked. Chords he plays, in sleep or standing, he
flicks his fingers, when idle or bored
flicks and when he's lost interest, he flicks again,
taps nail to nail, he picks a low baritone song, *Gratia Plena*.

Pelagic Cormorant

meaning "open sea"

The child tends to wander.
Takes his wooden dinghy, shoves off.
His mother makes him tie a line to the shore,
watches his oars lift and push,
feels a tug below her navel.
Doesn't see him catch a fish with his small net,
slice it and gut it and under his seat store it.
Doesn't see him loosen the knot,
bump the safety buoys
at the harbour's exit.

MATT BORCZON

For Jonah

When I
was gone
my youngest
son had
started having
issues that
finally needed
addressed with
a therapist
and suddenly
overnight
I was
reading emails
about the
Autism spectrum
and being
asked what
I thought
we should
do
I wish
I knew
then that
I was
so lost
in the
war
that my
own son
was just
another casualty
I bandaged
and moved
on from
like I

didn't know
Him
at all
everyone
had a
right to
hate me
my wife
for offering
her no
support
and no
empathy
Jonah for
my leaving
at a
time when
he needed
me
my other
3 kids
for having
to watch
my wife
do everything
learn everything
about PDD
about medicines
and prognosis
alone
while I
barely
remembered
to ask
in the
end all
I learned
about
Autistic
kids was
they didn't

like eye
contact or
to be
hugged
or want
to be
touched
so I
was surprised
when on
the first
night I
was back
he asked
me to
sleep in
his bed
asked to
lay his
head on
my shoulder

Jonah you
survived
this war
so much
better than
I did

KIM BRIDGFORD

A Crown for Sam

1.

I think of you as making music, still.

Because your oxygen was cut—not dead
Exactly—you decided, blue and impossible,
To believe in it, and lived. You never lied
Or had a mask, to make you better suited
For this life. You were just yourself.
                                        The lion
Pillow pet was the one you wanted, so you routed
Yourself, like a soldier, dragging your other one.
A dog? You could make a trade while others slept,
And did. Those days you were an actor, a sprite
Out of Shakespeare, born in February.
Out of a pattern of normalcy, you leapt
And made your own hip hop from albumed light.

Sometimes people disappointed, made you weary.

2.

Sometimes people disappointed, made you weary,
But that was the world. It also was Kanye West.
The thing that you liked most was empathy;
Yet you thought that people didn't like the loss
They felt when they met you. You had insight
That shaped your love; you used it to forgive.

Because you couldn't do what wasn't right.
Because you only had the moment's salve.
When you went through puberty—such a dark place—
You changed. Your sadness filled the pool of you.
Nothing to say. A gradual metamorphosis.

But still you had your family: your mother's face;
Your father, brother, sister's love. It was true:
Your clear devotion was the best of us.

3.

Your clear devotion was the best of us,
And sometimes you also experienced the worst.
At your elementary school, you waited, as
Your mother saw you, solitary, cursed
Because you'd bring the class's average down;
You sat in a wooden chair, principaled, during tests.
When your mother realized this—too late? too soon?—
What could be done to fix it? Because the final costs
Already could not be reckoned, or humane.

You moved, and started over there, with lightness.
You had an aide, and everything was new.
Is the word *idyllic?* Or was that just a sign
That, for a while, there was a pause, a brightness?
Your sister was a reader, as were you.

4.

Your sister was a reader, as were you.
You'd grow. You'd dream. You'd love rap music, lyrics.
You'd deepen in yourself, and, one day, you
Were nominated for Homecoming King. The storks
Don't usually drop their beaks with this bright basket:
And there you were. "Why did they pick *me?*" you asked.

Because you couldn't tell. Because the spot
Might have seemed to go to someone blessed
With an easier life. Because they wanted you.
Because they loved the way you loved them all.
Because the mums were swollen, bright, and open.
Because there are many ways this honor's due.
Because in the dimming light of turning fall
You stood for something, just about to happen.

5.

You stood for something, just about to happen.
And you went, with your mother, father, brother,
Sister, with your dress shirt, churchlike expectation.
People gathered under streamers, there together.
These were the days, as well, you worked so hard
To find a job that you could do. That night,
You loved the way your classmates, with the kindness card,
Under the streamers and the turning light,
Loved you.
            And may I now reveal the ending?
Because you won the kingship too. The crown.
Because you were as kind as they could be.
Because as representation of class and sending
Everyone into the world, you were their own:
What class should be, made of sincerity.

6.

What class should be, made of sincerity,
And balance, made out of friendship's aims
When everything was done from unanimity.
In happiness, you did a performance, rhymes
In a new song that you made in that moment.
This was one of the happiest times you'd had in life.
Because it showed how goodness felt, as it was lent,
By both the self and others.
                People still grieve
Many things about their lives. It is not perfect.
Sometimes there is a moment, made with love.
However, they loved the whole class, as they did you.
You looked at everyone with new respect.
For a moment, you were happy to believe.

Life moved on, and with it, so did you.

7.

Life moved on, and with it, so did you.
You built your life skills, played your music, all
With happiness, all with your patterns. Know
This about life: always paradoxical
And glorious. You loved your Rosie-cat,
But then you couldn't wake to go to class.
So you worked on everything. It's *this* for *that*.
It is the day-by-day of circumstance.

Your family grew. You then had a new brother,
And your elder brother became a school teacher
Because of you. We never know how all
The influences we have affect the other,
The rhapsodizing of what will one day reach there.

I think of you as making music, still.

EDWARD BYRNE

Seeking Inklings in an Old Video

He held mussel shells—indigo blue inside and black
on back—or those round pebbles he had

found rolling like dark marbles in the tidewater
wash, as if he had a handful of hard candy.

The wind's speed picked up, the sea shining behind
him, each wave displayed like a crinkled

sheet of tinfoil unfurled under that day's final
splay of sunlight. Every one of our son's

uneasy steps at the ocean's edge left an impression,
still refilling with water—even as I witness

it now, in midwinter three years later. We could
not have known then to watch for the few

symptoms we would soon learn to view with fear.
Even those little hints we missed, a lack

of balance whenever he would lean to lift another
stick of driftwood, as if the shoreline's

slant had suddenly become too steep, or the tipped
head and sideways glance he'd give us,

though we thought he only wanted reassurance,
were never seen as dubious sorts of acts

that ought to indicate a reason to have misgivings.
But to the two of us, now so suspicious,

feeling guilt, every unsure move that camera caught
appears to be uninvestigated evidence left

behind, even in this scene when the tape runs to its end.
He sits on the sand, back toward the shore,

counting out his collection of shells in a single file,
as if pretending every one of them were part

of some private treasure, the way anyone might
arrange family keepsakes, jewels or gems

kept as heirlooms somewhere in a darkened drawer,
brought out for comfort in a time of grief.

New Construction

In the distance, construction workers
hammer for hours at a new house

taking shape. Alex sits on our porch
and listens, softly nodding his head

under the slant of morning sunshine,
as if remembering steady drumbeats

of an old song or offering a private
signal of approval. When we walk

to watch the walls of the home rise
in late afternoon light, the second

floor nearly done, he shades his eyes
to peer up toward one of the higher

cut out places, as though he knows
a son like him will some night look

off from that bedroom, in the same
manner he does at times, and might

wonder about people passing below
or view the brighter stars far above,

attempting to gauge ways of worlds
always forming outside his window.

Learning Sign Language: "Yes"

1

Driving home from the post office,
we notice a stalk of black smoke growing,

rising from that blister of wreckage
in the distance, its far-off image dimly lit

by late daylight, the dying sunshine
hiding behind one fine line of cloud cover,

a dark couple of charred semis still
smoldering in the lingering heat of summer.

2

When we ask Alex whether he sees
this sign of damage hovering high above

the road ahead, my son, from whom
we've heard no more than a word or two

for four months, slowly folds fingers
into a fist (gesturing the way his mother

taught) as though to knock, hoping
for opening of an unseen door before him.

LAUREN CAMP

Adult Basic Education

Just after noon, a man in a hat wide as a boat
comes floating alone
to the Tutoring Center. His eyes fall

to the floor, but his voice keeps rocking, rowing—
into the vast waters of his bipolar

dyslexic mind, the rough waters
                            of his ADD mind;
the Asperger current constantly tugging him down.

Pulling out his pencil case, he anxiously organizes lead.
Pulling off his hat, he tangles his hair. He tangles
his language, tying up

vowels and consonants until he is holding a line of strange sounds
and a net
that sifts every surface.

A fleet of students sails past, propelled
by an endless schedule of classes. The man

        is becoming submerged
is submerged
in himself in the thrall of his worry is submerged
in the sinking.

I lead him to a small room and close the door.
His words dart away.

                            He lays his hat
                            on the table as the island
                            of knowing drifts by. Sweat washes
                            his forehead.

Trawling each murky blue-brown word, his search
streams in all directions.

I am learning the limited scope of his course,
the slant reckoning of position,
and how we must both keep him buoyed.

To settle the speed, he gathers the sail
of his panic, opens his book

to this week's vocabulary words:
                    anecdote, appreciate, believe, condone.

He looks off along the bottom of his mind,
tells me again about Asperger's.

                    "It's a form of optimism," he explains
and nerve cells miss the synapse:

he knows
what he means.

We begin riding the broad fin of language, finding our way
over the surface. We sound out
each alphabetical symbol: our C's crisp as fried kippers, each S extending
in curved lines down the coast of our tongues.

I say each word, and he hoists it up. I'm the one navigating
this trip because he's still leaving the harbor.
I'm the one tasked with pitching the rudder in the next logical direction.

Each word becomes a vessel
and we start to float
into the warm flow of paragraphs
in his *Sentence Skills* textbook. He's breathing better now.

When we've finished the hour, he's drained.
We've fished
                        for lost periods he can't always catch; we've angle
     for order, for every lesson in remembering.

Nothing is effortless, but we're both hooked
on language,

willing to sift deeper, and wash up again,

until, triumphant, we rise—

holding a word
or two

aloft.

The Dam of Asperger's

The boy's mind impounds |

whatever
comes near | each thought
laps the wall
and each
thought

recedes and spills

back
into the thick
harbor | self on self.

I wait for his answer,
watch it travel | the same slope
of *not thought.*

Seconds becomes sheets |
of this not thought.

The thought is not a shadow
not | a

not, but a passage | a knot of thought
and coordinates.
I notice

its particular sound | its
habitat of

volume and

each dip
down again as

his
mind floats with fluid |
sloshing the contour of

the thing I asked | as he sits listening to
some feature of the water

that I can't hear
on the side
of the wall | I can't reach.

Traveling with The Ferryman

I am damned close to the edge
because this golden Asperger's boy
was assigned a three-page term paper
on Purgatory. Rather than write it, he bites
his nails as I try to channel him through the grand
array of human experience. He wrenches his feet
back and forth. It's impossible to explain
that someday he too may be teetering
to a long ago gap. How can I say, *As you sway*
in hard-scrabble history, stay steady
for Cerberus and his rough rows of dark
teeth, the matted fur. Do not fear the crowding. Sit
pinned to night. He twirls his hair in his right hand.
He asks a pointless question, one filled with the enormity
of existence. I'm impatient, and he's in no hurry
to think through the future of his past. We pretend
his mind is not blurred with life's strongest
currents, that he knows lamentation and cold,
when instead he has changed course
to a track meet on Tuesday and his family's trip
to Alaska this summer—Will they see elk? From the endless
abyss, I nudge him and he scrutinizes
the window. We're reaching the irreducible
deadline. What will it take for him to hunch
in the innermost, to imagine he's in a stained boat
on a backdraft of previous days? *Oh, to hell with it!*
It's like having three heads, doing this tutoring job
with a boy in his reveries. Just as I give up, he looks to the side
without seeing, and says astrally *So…*, inching around
his unnavigable thoughts as he often does. He intones
with a voice thick and wrestled, *The ferryman will pull an obolus*
from our weeping eyes, showing each of our sins.
This 16-year-old on the verge of failing his classes
tells me, *We have to yield up our runneled faces.*
He shrugs and looks off. Then we sit in what is left
of winter, and the air seems fated with silence,
but still, it's made of air.

BARBARA CROOKER

Pushing the Stone

The stone
was heavy.
The family carried it
with them, all day.
Not one
could bear
its weight, alone.
Yet how they loved it.
No other stone had
its denseness,
its particular way
of bending the light.
They could not take
the stone
out in public,
had to keep it home,
let it sing songs
in its own strange language,
syllables of schist and shale.
When the mother's back ached,
the father took the stone
for a while, then passed it
from sister to sister.
The stone
became a part of them,
a bit of granite
in the spine,
a shard of calcite
in the heart.
Sometimes
its weight
pressed them
thin, transparent
as wildflowers
left in the dictionary.

Sometimes
it was
lighter
than air.
The stone
did not talk.
But it shone.

The Children of the Challenger League Enter Paradise

(The Challenger League is the handicapped division of Little League USA)

Here in Little League heaven,
there will be no strikes against you
before you're up at bat,
no standards and regulations
to struggle against, no segregation,
no special education.
All the empty wheelchairs, braces, walkers.
No seat belts, head supports, drool bibs.
The crooked, straight. The rough places, plains.
No toy bats, wobbly tees, wiffle balls,
everybody-scores-outs-don't-count-rules.
These are the Major Leagues, stadium packed,
bases loaded, and the lights are on in the firmament.
Samantha winds up to pitch. David hits
a hard line drive deep to center. Adam
throws to Trevor, straight and true.
But here comes Jodie, stealing second,
then third, no longer held aloft by her dad,
while her legs windmill in the dust, no,
she's faster than the ink on a new contract,
she's sliding into home,
her smile bright enough
to power Detroit.

Washing Diapers

The last woman in America to wash diapers
lugs the full pail down to the first floor,
heaves it in the washer, makes it spin its offal load.
How many diapers has she sloshed in the toilet,
how many neatly folded stacks has she raised skyward,
soft white squares of cotton, pieces of cloud,
how many double and triple folds has she pinned
on little bottoms? How many nights
of checking beds did she find those buns
raised in the air, loaves resting on a bakery shelf?
She knows the power of bleach, the benefits of rinsing.
On winter nights, when the snow comes down
in glittery drifts, she sees Ivory Flakes,
their slippery iridescence. When it comes
to dealing with the shit in her life,
nothing else is so simple, so white, so clean.

Grating Parmesan

A winter evening,
sky, the color of cobalt,
the night coming down like the lid on a pot.
On the stove, the ghosts of summer simmer:
tomatoes, garlic, basil, oregano.
Steam from the kettle rises,
wreathes the windows.
You come running when I reach for the grater,
"Help me?" you ask, reversing the pronouns,
part of your mind's disordered scramble.
Together, we hold the rind of the cheese,
scrape our knuckles on the metal teeth.
A fresh pungency enters the room.
You put your fingers in the fallen crumbs:
"Snow," you proudly exclaim, and look at me.
Three years old, nearly mute,
but the master of metaphor.
Most of the time, we speak without words.

Outside, the icy stones in the sky
glitter in their random order.
It's a night so cold, the very air freezes flesh,
a knife in the lungs, wind rushing
over the coil of the planet
straight from Siberia,
a high howl from the wolves of the steppes.
As we grate and grate, the drift rises higher.
When the family gathers together,
puts pasta in their bowls,
ladles on the simmered sauce,
you will bless each one
with a wave of your spoon:
"Snowflakes falling
all around."
You're the weatherman
of the kitchen table.
And, light as feathers,
the parmesan sprinkles down,
its newly fallen snow
gracing each plate.

Autism Poem: The Grid

A black and yellow spider hangs motionless in its web,
and my son, who is eleven and doesn't talk, sits
on a patch of grass by the perennial border, watching.
What does he see in his world, where geometry
is more beautiful than a human face?
Given chalk, he draws shapes on the driveway:
pentagons, hexagons, rectangles, squares.
The spider's web is a grid,
transecting the garden in equal parts.

Sometimes he stares through the mesh on a screen.
He loves things that are perforated:
toilet paper, graham crackers, coupons
in magazines, loves the order of tiny holes,
the way boundaries are defined. And real life
is messy and vague. He shrinks back to a stare,
switches off his hearing. And my heart,
not cleanly cut like a valentine, but irregular
and many-chambered, expands and contracts,
contracts and expands.

Simile

My autistic son showed me his paper
from remedial English; he was supposed
to fill in the blanks: Cool as a _____.
Smooth as a _____. Neat as a _____.

He came up with: angry as a teakettle,
and when I asked, "Why? "said, "Because
it was boiling mad." Of course,
it was marked wrong, one more red mark
in his life's long test.

When I called from Virginia to ask him
what he did last weekend,
he said, "We bought Italian salad dressing."
I tell my writing students to focus
on the one inch square.

Last fall, we went to a Broadway play;
what he liked the most
were the traffic lights and *Don't Walk* signs.

Oh, my little pork chop, my sweet potato, my tender tot.
You have made me pay attention to the world's smallest
minutia. My pea-shaped heart, red as a stop sign,
swells, fills with the helium of tenderness, thinks it might burst.

One Word

When I told my friend from college that my son
was autistic, she said, "Why, that's wonderful. Does
he paint or draw?" And my mother, at eighty-nine,
still tries to hold on, keep the thin thread
of cognition wound around her finger,
but can't find her words: "You know what I mean,"
she tells me, "It's that thing that goes with the wash."
I play along, use Twenty Questions: "Large or small
box? Solid or Liquid?" until I find out she's talking
about dryer sheets. Then there's that game
that used to appear in the Sunday papers,
where you changed one letter at a time
to create a new word at the end. So *dime*
becomes *dome* becomes *tome* becomes *tomb*.
So the afternoon leaks its light out, a letter at a time.
Seated at the round table, I *eat* toast with my mother,
make *tea*. Such a slight subtraction, for *love*
to turn to *lose*.

LISA M. DOUGHERTY

The Dead Tree Garden

She is pacing, as she normally does, waiting for the school bus. Today it is outside, the weather being a bit warmer. And suddenly she remembers it is supposed to be spring now. The garden beds are still *barren*. A word I accidentally dropped in conversation and had to explain the meaning of. The bus is still not here. So she begins picking up twigs. Holding them up she notices they are like small replicas of the trees still without leaves. Admires their nakedness. And so she wants to keep them, begins to plant them in the soft soil, chattering and telling me when I try to stop her that, she knows they will not grow. The bus is late again. She is finished, and stands up proud of what she has just done. If they don't come soon I will have to take her in. Avoid off-setting her day should she miss breakfast. She likes to eat with the other kids. She is smiling, telling me it is her "Dead Tree Garden." And so it is. And the bus isn't going to get here in time. I run to grab my keys, I look back at her and her garden of dead trees. I don't tell her that the wind will soon blow it down.

Alongside

For my daughter Amara and her best friend Kyrah

To school she wears long sleeves
And slips on her knit gloves to avoid
The unwanted feel of paper.
She crawls off her bed
Sleeping by the air vent
Beneath a tent made
Of her comforter, stripped down
To undergarments
Just enough to keep
The feel of a constant
Cool on her exposed skin.
Goes into immediate
Retreat at the mention of a hug,
Climbing her voice
Against the undesired touch.
Stretches her cuffs
Beyond the length of fingertip
To practice formation
With her ice-skating partner.
But she has a friend
On a different end
Of a brilliant spectrum,
Equally radiant with
Both smiles and affirmations,
Her own determination.
So today someone stomps
Another foot
Asserting the hardwood
Echoes in my direction.
Still there's only one name
She has ever
Intentionally recalled. With the way
My memory purposely holds on,
The way with her forgetful
About anything else mind,
She's held on
Almost 5 years now,

To the only one I've ever seen,
With whom she walks alongside,
Nothing getting in between
Them and with what
Their bare hands hold
Together.

Ascribe

A shoe grazes the floor and *scuffs* its way into a language against her.
When the flying grass-hopper jumps trying to open its wings against
the lid of an emptied Cool Whip container, is then, *desperation* not
a sound. Do the ears of an autistic child not multiply into the same
factor of what perspective a bee's eye makes into our distortion.
What she hears different when a chair is pulled out in the kitchen,
she can only name as an assault directly set into wavelength. *Screech*,
I imagine was named for the way she'd tear through the seemingly
quiet. *Enough.* She waves a white flag with her fingers pressed into
the side of her head as her feet *pound* for *pound* her path up the
stairs to where she can not run any further away. And yet, the sky.
The same sky she would point her little finger to and draw the *ooh*
out of the moon. When it sounds as if it could *break* sound. *Asleep*, is
a sound, I listen through the cracked door for. The sky, it does not
wake her.

She Talks in Muddy Puddles

Sometimes as the rain falls
Softly into the dips
Of when she used to let us
Hold her up for a picture
Smiling her wayward curls
As she'd press her face
To a cheek's touch.
Something less delicate
A too much pondered child,
Curiously set to motion
But aware of the danger
Of touching a moth's wing.
Or when she let
Her clothes match
As we had walked out
Towards the falling sky,
Before she did not want told
How pretty she was,
Daunting ladybug
Boots and matching parka.
Her mind too busy
Trying to negate things,
Or navigate
As she stomped mud
From the pooled
Miniature wetlands
Between the strips of grass
And the asphalted road.
What she questioned
Was more her,
And the right to ask
Not for a long lecture
Or the answer to,
She was always
Closer than we thought.
As for the questions she asked
I tried to rinse out then,
Only now realizing
It was stiffness

She wanted nothing of,
A stark resolution for her
Would never be stomped out
Where small lakes are
Big enough
Two small feet could find
The bottom fast.
As she skipped
Past all the puddles
Of clear water. Never
Standing still.

Ask of the Feather You Found on the Ground

Did you not want to be part
Of what flies? What finds
The current to ride
Effortless through the air?
Ask what you broke
De-fleshing yourself from
The natural pattern, of something
For you. I pour another glass
In the bird-bath of ice and whisky.
Bathe long after the sun
Feathers the sky the color of after-birth.
And you think because you are the gray
Too often gazed on by, that maybe
You are not something uniquely taken,
Flighted from the path of a spectrum
Not quite defined. Ask if it is not
Something, that you've been
Thrown off of
The balance this left
Wing
Has relied on.

Autism On the Earth's Delicate Carpet

She tilts her head to one shoulder
And covers her other ear
To write, the sound of a pencil
Is like scratching paper.
And the meltdown
Should she have to erase
More homework than usual tonight.
So I let her take a break out back,
With the condition of bare feet.
And she just lays in the shaded grass
With her shirt lifted over her belly
To feel the coolness
Of the earth's delicate carpet.
At least today she is not in a pace'
Walking the house with her animal
And bumping it into her head.
There is air spray in every room
In case a bad smell.
Because she knows me making
Her favorite muffins
When I'm still mixing in the bowl.
So please don't let them sit her
Next to the kid who farts a lot in class.
She will be honest and extreme!
And yet she tells me things
Like did I know, butterflies
Have taste-buds on their feet?
Or will ask me in a bath how
The tub is liquid with water
That is really two gasses? And why
Doesn't blowing air bubbles change it?
She dries off and gets ready for bed,
Cuddles up shirtless by the air vent
Then puts her feet under the bed
To fall asleep on the floor.
It's her world of small spaces
Her feelings of safeness.
And I get to keep these small moments of her,
When beyond all her questionings

She turns on her music
And we say our *I Love You's*,
It's always, *Can you lay with me?*
And then I just listen to her,
Sometimes still chatting away,
Or, just breathing.

Sean Thomas Dougherty

Dear Editor of Poetry Journals Named After Famous Cities

I am writing to ask, have you ever eaten a cloud? You see my youngest daughter didn't use the toilet till she was after 4 years old. She'd shit in a diaper and didn't seem to mind. She refused to read till she was six though she spent hours flipping the pages of books and speaking out her made-up stories, but then what stories are not made up? Or her speech impediment, and the battery of tests on her brain. But today the sun was warm along the great lake. They call this weather Indian Summer, the red leaves and light. We were out on the back porch when our daughter reached up with her forked fingers as if to pluck the sky and turned and chewed, "I ate a cloud, dada, I ate a cloud!" Have you ever eaten a cloud, dear editor? You don't seem like the type, who has done this, with your Ivy degrees and serious statements on art. And what does a cloud taste like? Well, my daughter says, "Love. A cloud it tastes like love."

CHERYL DUMESNIL

Moon, Jacket, Yellow, Tree, Violin

My two-year-old son loves words—
apple, umbrella, octopus—anything

he can spell, type, or read. He bathes
with two foam alphabets floating

in the soapy water, arranges wet letters
on the faux marble wall, sounding out

melon, mama, x-ray, ice cream.
From the backyard swing, he sees

B, C, and *K* spelled out in the craggy
bare branches of the walnut tree.

And when I'm anchored to the couch,
nursing his infant brother, he drags

a magnetic drawing board over
by its string-attached pen, demanding,

"Mommy, write *watermelon.*" How can I
refuse a kid afflicted with my own

addiction? So with my less-than dexterous
left hand, I scratch it out, upside down,

for him to read. "Now *piano*," he says,
wiping the slate clean. And then

I hand over the pen, "Your turn, buddy."
Concentration wrinkles his brow, the tip

of his tongue peeks out the corner of his lips
as he draws the illegible letters, whispering

F . . I . . . S . . . H, each shaky line
a new boat unmoored from its dock.

Before bedtime, he climbs up
on my office chair, lifts the hood of the laptop

to type the day's list of favorites:
moon, jacket, yellow, tree, violin.

He prints this verbless poem and stores it
in a red folder on his bookshelf, along

with the others. As I sing him to sleep,
more constellations of letters form

in his brain, while my own words wait,
winter carp under a ceiling of ice.

Teaching Luca Mr. Potato Head

He taps the floor with splayed fingers,
shakes his autistic moon face at the ceiling's

florescent bulbs, marble blue eyes
cocked right. I'm supposed to teach him

to play appropriately, so I unlatch
the storage box lid and place two plastic

potato torsos on the carpet between us,
then spill a salad of lime green, pink, red

and white body parts by Luca's folded leg.
I loop my thumb and pointer around

his bird bone wrist, brush his palm
across the brown plastic form. "Do this,"

I say, taking a clam-shaped ear from the pile,
sliding its stem in the spud's side hole.

He tilts his head to scan the toy, lifts it
to his wet mouth and grunts agreement.

Then the boy's brain rattles into my world
long enough to pick a white arm and

plant it in his doll's coned head. Together
we become minor gods, our hands

clawing the spare parts pile until my doll
stands, like the sample picture's twin,

on blue sneaker feet, green backpack
slung over its crooked elbow, and Luca

has sculpted Picasso's dream—waxy lips
talking out the ear hole, google eyes

in place of teeth, antennae arms raised
to grasp satellite words. Luca gives his beast

a drooling smile, then rotates his wrists
to sign "All done." I wouldn't change a thing.

American Robin

—the first bird to pipe up
after the rain clouds shut off

for the day. At work,
I show my client a flashcard

and say, *This is a Robin.*
He says, *No it's not, it's a bird.*

He speaks in the block language
of cardboard picture books,

and I try to fill in the gaps,
holding up Macaw and Blue Jay

and Black Bird for him to learn.
What nuances get lost when

we don't have the language
to name them—the Inuit's

mythical hundred words
for *snow,* versus our functional

descriptions: powdery, wet, icy,
the kind that makes good

snowballs, the kinds that don't.
How that notion of one hundred

descriptors makes us want to see
more, to look for distinctions

between the lacy flakes that rest
on a scarf and the white asterisks

that freeze in the corners of your
window on a sub-zero night.

When I ask him, *What should we
play today?* He replies, *I want*

to play with...a something,
and I remember a time when

my own answers to the question,
How do you feel? began

with the phrase, *I think...*
How the mind overlooks

the waves of the body, until
we learn the words to name them.

I sing "Little Robin Red Breast"
while he cuts feather shapes

out of colored paper. We write
a word on each feather

and glue it to his wings.

Vocabulary

Snaking between backyard fences
        of million dollar homes, Las Trampas
                Creek has swallowed a two-slice

chrome toaster and a yellow bike
        with a wire basket like newspaper
                delivery boys used to ride. My kid,

climbing the bridge railing, says,
        Small airplanes have straight wings
                pointing left and right, or east and west.

Yes, I say, that's called perpendicular
        to the fuselage. Always I want to offer him
                something lasting and good, but today

all I've got is vocabulary. So he rolls those
        pebbles of sound around in his mouth
                while we watch two Canada geese

move like captain-less clipper ships, cutting
        S-patterns through green water, and then
                a county bus rushes by, sending eddies

of fallen oak leaves spiraling down
        the sidewalk, like a herd of drunk beetles,
                and we walk home under an archway

of wind-stripped branches, distant
        call of that migrating flock bugling
                toward us, ripping open the winter-dark sky.

VIVIAN EDEN

Form and Grace

In a move as formal
as entering Switzerland
we brought you to the new school.
The children had meandering
smiles and random eyes.
You were the most beautiful
and the only Jew.
For two weeks you flourished
intermittently bright like
the mallards in November.
The nurses suggested
there might be some mistake.
But child, you never let us forget
that form, that grace
can't always suffice.

SUSAN ELMSLIE

After the diagnosis I went to the pool to ease into cold fact

for Wes

Tell me joy persists. I need that to hold
as I parse the lengthening shadows:
therapies, special schools, the thinning hope
that he may speak, ride a bike, beat the odds.

You were back at home, resting with our son.
And just when I should have been packing up,
I caught sight of a Chinese kite, a dragon,
red, swooping in the wind and so high up

I thought it must have broken free, lost.
"Look, someone's kite escaped!" a boy exclaimed,
pointing skyward. There the kite danced, wind-tossed,
too high to think it held by any hand.

Yet, buoyed, I watched it for a good long time,
until I felt the nature of the rhyme.

Broken Baby Blues

Can I say it to myself, I've got the broken baby blues?
Can I say it to the wind, I've got the broken baby blues?
Listen to me sister, walk a mile in my shoes.

My baby's perfect but his brain won't let him talk.
Said my baby's perfect but his brain won't let him talk.
A doctor helped my baby learn to walk.

I feared before his birth that something might go wrong.
When we stitched him in the womb I feared something might go wrong.
Now I fear for myself because I'm singing this song.

I love my sweet baby and I want to do him right.
Yes, I love my sweet baby and I aim to do him right.
Don't know how to mend his ills—I'm living darkest night.

Ain't no mama nowhere safe from broken baby blues.
No daddy—God in heaven!—hasn't paid his dues.
Lord God save my baby from the broken mama blues.

Happy Blues

*A "blue note" is a note from outside of a given tonality which gives that
tonality (or chord, etc.) a dissonant "bite." Most blue notes come from the
vocal practice (later imitated by horn players and guitarists) of "sliding"
into notes from either a half step above or below rather than landing right
on them, which produces a "dirty" or "bluesy" sound which most often
resolves to the "correct" note from within the tonality.*
—Durrlman Hesse

We want to leave you happy, / Don't want to leave you sad.
—Ella Fitzgerald

It hits me: there should be video of my son while he's not having a
seizure or collapsing, marionette-like, in episodic ataxia. Something
not for the doctors but for us, something that, when we watch it
months later, elicits a comparatively uncomplicated joy.

Dues, one and two
Dues, doesn't matter nothing

So this time, I film him while he's playing, sure of his grip on the
disk-shaped beads, which he stacks on pegs set into a wooden base,
following what must be his own sense of order. He's four, atypical.
His sense of order is beads jumbled, mouthed, dropped on the
floor.

Dues, three and four
Dues, maybe more, that's all right

I film him as he says, "on, om, on on," and slides beads onto a
peg. On the tallest peg he slides two red pentagons, a green circle,
followed by two more reds, capped by a blue square. Then he turns
it upside down to begin again. Now blue first on the red peg. Then
he brings the toy to his mouth as though taking a sip from red's
blue spout.

I've sung these blues, and I'm through
Cause I don't know what I'm singing about

Look, he's put four red pentagons together—capped by a green
circle on the red peg. Albers' colour studies dance in my mind's
eye. I film for 34 seconds and have to stop to pick up the blue bead
that fell when he mouthed the toy. He'd leaned over the side of his
trip-trap chair, reaching for blue, saying "Help me, help me." "Get
it?" I asked. And he looked at me, repeated, "Geddee," happy to be
understood.

I am happy you are happy too
I am happy you are happy too

Watching and re-watching our video together, we're transfixed.
He glances down at his chest, tugs at his Gap t-shirt, recognizing
it from the clip. Every time we hear the bead drop in our record-
ed scene, in reply to my line, "Get it?" he answers again, out loud,
"Geddee," in sync with the boy in the video grasping the toy, look-
ing at the floor and then over at his mom, who replies, "I'll get it,
hold on."

So let's go out with the blues that's swinging
Like Count Basie, swing on
Like Count Basie, swing on
Like Count Basie, swing on
Like Count Basie, swing on
Swing on, swing out tonight

Quick

"That's enough! How can you let him get away with that?"
I hear a woman shout at my husband near the Pik-Nik.
Our son has screamed one too many times,
band-saw-on-steel-pipe screams. Who hasn't heard
such a child? From the shoe store, where I've the cushier job
of helping our daughter pick out sneakers, I heard him,
thrashing in my husband's grasp, stomping, going Jell-O
trying to break free, to hurtle through the mall.

                           He's five.
For him, words are balloons that have floated away.
Running came late and he wants to keep it.

"I'm sorry ma'am, he may not look like it,
but this is a special-needs child," my husband says,
in a tone I would call even, if I didn't know better.
There's no adjective for this inflection. Call it
river otter versus crocodile. One of many
leaves falling from the oak.
                     The Chinese word *Téng*—
to love—said by a parent to a child
uses the same character as *to hurt*.

From the store's entrance, I can see the woman
and her burly partner dry-erase the air
around their fast-food trays. "Sorry, never mind,"
they both say, as though they'd tried to order breakfast
after the lunch menu went up.

I drift back to my daughter, who's sinking
in a quicksand of shoes.

We reunite with the boys,
drop some loonies into mechanical ponies.
Cross the parking lot together.
"The cashier at the wine store said, 'Some people
are such jerks'," my husband offers, quietly,
hands square on the wheel, and it is consoling.

Are thicker skins on sale at Reitman's?
Will I shop online?
A glass of wine might not be enough
for me, the brooder who'll replay, replay, replay
the rebuke ricocheted around the mall,
hovering its mirror inches from everyone's nose. Cut
to my son who has to hear
his father offer this defense to a stranger.
The unnameable tone.

Tone comes from the Greek for *to stretch*—
a reaching towards or a pulling away.
Shouldn't we be used to it by now?

Alive

A flame we have tended,
cupping our hands around him,
our backs to the wind.

From the earliest days
EEG showed abnormal activity.
Misfiring neurons. Meds

tamped the seizures
so that he might advance,
reach milestones.

Some milestones he has met.
Others tumbled as scree
down a steep slope.

We say *We love you!*
You are strong!
Leap up!

And when he leaps
we say *bravo*! Or *danger*!
because he knows no fear

will not hear *no,*
does not sleep, driven
to pull the tree down

smash mirrors, family photos,
swallow the glass, everything
in his mouth. Your hair,

my arm. Seven years on
and we tend, turning
our frazzled hours to his needs

and sleeping, when permitted,
like logs, like dried timber.
He gets stronger. See

how he licks the walls,
turns direction unpredictably
on the stairs. We tend this blaze,

every day,
every day willing
to be burned. Every day

alive.

Grass

> *O I perceive after all so many uttering tongues!*
> —Walt Whitman, "A child said, What is the grass?"

"Grass," I said, plopping down in the park.
"Grass," Magnus said,
squatting to pat it with his palms.
He was two.
Since then, four seasons of grass, fresh cut,
browning and strewn with leaves, have passed.
Grass was a one-time word, one of many
one-time words that grew and were mown,
scattered to the wind. Yet we held it once—
damp and green and ordinary.

Rebecca Foust

Dark Card

When they look at my son like that
at the grocery store check out
or at school assemblies,
I wait for the right moment, till they move
through laughter, raised eyebrows, clamped lips
—but before fear. Then I switch gears,
go into my tap dance-and-shuffle routine.

Yes, he's different, all kids are different, him
just a little bit more—oh, he's knocked down
the applesauce pyramid? So sorry, here,
my sleeves conceal napkins for messes like this,
and I can make them disappear. But before
I do, make sure you marvel at how the jars
made an algorithm when he pulled that one free.

Oh, he was standing on his desk again, crowing
like a rooster in your third-period class?
Yes, bad manners, and worse luck
that he noticed how today's date and the clock
matched the hour of what you taught
last week in a footnote—the exact pivotal
second of the Chinese Year of the Cock.

Before they get angry, I pull out my deck, deal
out what they want. Yes, he's different,
but look at his IQ score, his Math SAT!
I've figured out that difference pays freight
when linked with intelligence; genius trumps odd,
and alchemizes bizarre into merely eccentric.
So I play the dark card of the idiot savant,

trotting out parlor tricks in physics and math:
he sees solutions the way you might breathe!
Or perceive! The color green! It's my ploy

to exorcise their pitchforks and torches,
to conjure Bill Gates when they see him,
or Einstein, not Kaczynski or Columbine;
perhaps they'll think him delightfully odd

or oddly delightful, dark Anime eyes,
brow arc calligraphy on rice paper skin,
his question mark flowerstalk spine.
But it's a swindle, a flimflam, a lie,
a not-celebration of what he sees
with his inward-turned eye:
the patterns in everything—traffic, dirt piles,

bare branches of trees, matrices in jar stacks,
Shang Dynasty history in tick of school clock,
music in color and math, the way shoppers
shuffle their feet while waiting on line;
how he tastes minute differences between brands—
even batches-within-brands—of pickles and cheese;
how he sees the moonlit vole
on the freeway's blurred berm.

Perfect Target

—how they'd leer when he walked up
to them with his face flower-open, then
one would shrug a book-ballasted backpack
to sprawl him out flat on the asphalt.

How they'd tell him that the teacher
wanted, no really wanted him to jump
on the lunch table to see if it would break,
the apology note after note after note

he dutifully wrote. How at bath time
he'd say the bruises and scrapes were
nothing, nothing, leave it alone,
Mom, don't make it worse Mom.

How one time they cornered him
behind the storage shed and stoned him
in a hail of green oranges, leaving him
facedown bloodsnotted in dirt.

How he braided in three strands the lanyard
of his middle school years;
the hours and hours spent pacing
the playground alone,

the play dates and parties
he was never invited to, the chairs
pulled away
just before he sat down.

He Never Lies

not because he won't
or doesn't know better,
or how, he just can't.
I imagine him telling
too much of a truth,
or hell-bent on one
of his endless, spiraling,
descending dissents,

I fear he'll be over-blunt
or otherwise by accident
draw their attention,
annoyance, and rage.
How far might they go
to assuage
their discomfort with difference?

I imagine him drugged
or locked down on a ward;
in my nightmare
he's caged.

Eighteen

Maybe I don't have to whisk
the ice smooth ahead of your
curling stone, explain
how you don't always mean

what you say, nor say what
you mean; tell why you don't cry
even though you feel pain,
explain your indifference

to rain. Or sun. How when
you get wet, sometimes
you burn. You're learning
to manage on your own,

how to keep track of taking
your meds, where and when
to get more, how much
and whether you took them

today. You're beginning
to take time from screen time
to eat, brush your teeth
and shave your luxurious beard,

you remember to set your
alarm. Charge your phone
in case your friends call.
Your friends. Your friends call.

Show Your Work

My son is not good at emotion,
or doing things
to ease understanding;
he does not usually notice
when people are displeased.

In preschool, his peers absorbed
social hierarchies
and nonverbal cues, but
he showed a preference
for algorithms.

In math class he got D's
for not showing his work.
He must have cheated,
because no one can understand
a theorem without proving it,

especially not the teachers
who taught him the discipline
of showing his work;
hours spent sitting with
the slow, wayward pencil

gripped at an odd angle,
to lay down the evidence
for what he'd grasped in a breath.
Years later, he told me
all that work was made-up,

what he imagined the rest of us
needed to find the solution
that came to him whole,
unbidden, like a horizon moon.

I don't do math, so in my mind
the work he showed
goes like this:

(-) small-talking
(-) planning
(-) reviewing your day
(-) worrying about the thousand details
that do not concern this problem

+ look inward
+ get up from your chair
+ walk through the dark house to the back door
+ find the latch and slide the bolt
+ walk into the clarity and stillness
of the dark night air where

_____

= it is possible to look up and stare
at an infinity of moon.

Homage to Teachers

Ring the bell for Ms. Ruto,
gentle and neutral when she described
him sitting on the first-grade rug

facing *this way* while the rest
of the class faced *that way*;
Ring it for Doc, who piled desk

on desk in the room's center
and let the kids climb up to sail their
own Mayflower, who grinned

at our conferences, saying
you've got a live one! Ring
the bell for Ms. Stone, who

debunked the acronym disorders—
ADHD, ODD, OCD—*saying school
is the problem; he needs to be*

*John Muir roaming the fields
with binoculars, and he's trapped
in my class room.*

And ring a last carillon
for Dr. Hart, who took him aside
in high school Chem to confide

that her brain worked exactly like
his brain worked, then made him her TA,
the job coveted by Honors Students

applying to Stanford, but for my son
the reason he finished high school,
and learned how to set his alarm.

The Peripheral Becomes Crucial

in ways we'd never have guessed, like when
they unwound the crocodile-mummy shroud
focusing on what was within,

casting aside as trash the papyri cartonnage,
which when kicked, unscrolled to reveal
what Sappho wrote.

Sometimes more is inscribed
in the chemical signature of mud
than in the Sanskrit writ on the pot.

My son is gentler with moths
than people ever were with him,
and he chooses truth like breath.

He sets out cutlery backwards at table,
every time; he shaman-finds the bird point
flint, the fish spine, the speckled egg.

We watch as the linen-strip, tight-wrap coil
of that Gordian-knot neck-throttled curse,
that gene-encrypted, linked-chain curse,

that DES-taken-by-grandmother curse,
that fumble-fingered-fool-doctor-shaped curse,
unravels with his years, unwinds, unfolds,

lets loop out in vast uncoiling spirals
whole archives of text, found worlds.

an autist's mother reflects

afraid to die
before you

but in this wild
dark New Hampshire

meadow   fireflies
glow like downed pulsars

all incandescence
like your face

& no trace of errant gene
or what perished

to breed such rapture light

JENNIFER FRANKLIN

Gift

The eight-year-old chemo
patient in line for the swings
was sad for you—how you

screamed with a sob so loud
it scattered pigeons from the patch
of dirt around all the swings,

though there was still food
to forage. She asked me why
there was no medicine of any kind

in *the whole hospital* that could
cure you. She gave you her swing
even though she was next and had

only an hour outside. She asked
me if she could push you and I
could not refuse her kindness. *Swinga*

me, swinga me, you shrieked.
I don't know how long we stood
together, listening to your

delirious laughter, distracted
by flight. When you decided
you'd had enough, you lay

your hand on her bald head while you stood.
She tried to comfort me, and
offered you a little bear a nurse had given her,

but you handed it back without looking
at it. She had already given you
the only thing you wanted.

Burial of the Brains, Vienna 2002

In front of reporters and doctors, dignitaries parade
seven hundred brains of children in black urns.

Sixty years after Dr. Gross killed them with poisoned
cocoa and starvation, their bodies are finally left

alone. Awarded the cross of honor for his research
on gray matter of the children he murdered—

epileptics, autistics, midgets—citizens of the city
still protect him. My love, you would have been

among the first taken—force-fed and when you
vomited, force-fed your vomit, your head then pushed

into the toilet and flushed and told to *wash your face*
as the doctors did to all girls who survived.

Your shrieks and babble would have been smothered.
You couldn't have suffered frostbitten toes in silence.

Throughout the funeral, youth of Vienna, ashamed
of their ancestors' past, hold posters of the lovely

little faces. Most are younger than you are now.
Seven hundred children labeled, sliced onto slides,

stored in jars for sixty years. Studied until 1998.
Why does cruelty require so much time for clarity?

I fold myself in the corner of my mauve room
with a prayer box full of stashed pills. Even when

you don't wake screaming, I can't sleep
because of what you'll suffer when I am gone.

While Waiting, *Godot* Interrupts

Sometimes, I ask questions I know
you will not answer. Like if you feel sick

or if our ancestors invented cave painting
or song first. You never lie to me

because you do not speak. How can I
still believe in language—do words

have more weight than those bags we carry?
Have meaning? You could think me

an ignorant fool for believing. You
could think. The behaviorists tell me

your tears do not mean you're in pain—
neither psychic nor physical. That crying's

a habit to pass time like hamsters
running a wheel or shopping for clothes

we don't need. We go on, alone, together—
our arms intertwined—nothing if not love.

Your warm face, fat with life, is not afraid
of the dark or any other usual thing,

though the sound of certain words (lake,
Daddy, doctor) are enough to pin you

to the floor in fear. When you hear them,
you scream "take it off" as if words

were masks one can wear to undo us.
Still, we both speak some lines in this

little dwelling—our own ditch and tree.
Every spring the palm pretends it's dying—

yellow leaves waving like arms conducting
a desperate SOS and overnight, improbable,

six new shoots. You line things up, spin,
and skip across the room. When you

allow me, I play Bach ("No thank you,
please") as I try to divert you with songs

and little stories "Too much, too much."
Sometimes you noose thick rope

around my neck; other times, I do.
Maybe it would be better if we parted.

Mostly, you take charge. People tell me
you're happier than most. That you're blessed,

like some animal on the farm—a pig—
ignorant of her own impending doom.

You stand on one leg, your lovely body
contorted in unnatural shapes. When

you're happy you're happy. When you cry
you're not, whatever the doctors claim.

The walls and river must be terribly bored
watching us. The moment you walk through

the door you take siege of this place.
With only time before us, I try to teach you

to wash yourself, to put on your own boots.
If we parted? That might be better for us.

When you fall asleep, I cover you with green wool.
Every day, we wake and plot our escape. No longer

safe to take you outside alone, the prison
of our apartment—no longer figurative—

"I'm all done." Everything you know
of the world, you discover from one bay window.

We can still part if you think it would be better.
If we could exist apart from each other.

Talking to My Daughter after Beckett

With the bell, I wake and talk to myself—
so little one can say and yet one must

say all. I don't blame you when you
ignore me. I'm grateful for the *wonderful*

mercies and say *you are a darling today,*
darling. Each day, I mean it. Consider

a mirror—give me life without illusion.
A bag, a toothbrush, a music box, a song

that must *rise up from the heart like a thrush.*
"You can do it," I say as you wake. "We did it,"

I reassure you when we complete each day.
It is a mistake to sing too early. I reveal what

saved me, why I wrap it as I would a gift.
Remind me how to speak without being heard

and yet speak more—until the bell.
Until we are buried both of us, in sand.

My Daughter's Body

If you saw her, you would think she was beautiful.
Strangers stop me on the street to say it.

If they talk to her they see that this beauty
Means nothing. Their sight shifts to pigeons

On the sidewalk. Their eye contact becomes
As poor as hers. They slip away slowly,

With varying degrees of grace. I never know
How much to say to explain the heartbreak.

Sometimes, I tell them. More often,
I remain silent. As her smile sears me, I hold

Her hand all the way home from the swings.
The florist hands her a dying rose and she holds it

Gently without ripping the petals like she does
To the tulips that stare at us with their insipid faces,

Pretending that they can hold my sorrow
In their outstretched cups because I knew them

Before I knew grief. They do not understand that
They are ruined for me now. I planted five hundred

Bulbs as she grew inside of me, her brain already
Formed by strands of damaged DNA

Or something else the doctors don't understand.
After her bath, she curls up on me for lullabies—

The only time during the day that her small body is still.
As I sing, I breathe in her shampooed hair and think

Of the skeletons in the *Musée de Préhistoire*
In Les Eyzies. The bones of the mother and baby

Lie in a glass case in the same position we are
In now. They were buried in that unusual pose,

Child curled up in the crook of the mother's arm.
The archaeologists are puzzled by the position.

It doesn't surprise me at all. It would be so easy
To die this way—both of us taking our last breaths

With nursery rhymes on our open lips
And the promise of peaceful sleep.

I Would Like My Love to Die

after Beckett

I would like my love to die
Or at least that I didn't love you

So much. If I could turn my heart
To winter, I wouldn't need to do this

To the earth. If you didn't smile
In your sleep or touch my face

With tenderness, I could walk away
From you when you left through

The trap door of my hosta-lined heart
Without looking back.   I wish I didn't love

You so much. I would like my love to die
So I wouldn't have to murder everything

Around me. So I wouldn't have to be
The hunter I have become. But you're

Not going to release me from your unnatural
Embrace. You pin me beside you with your

Thin arm around my neck. It doesn't look
Strong enough to hold a small animal; but it is.

SHERINE GILMOUR

Injection #3: Compounded Folinic Acid and Subcutaneous Methylcobalamin

Poor sweetheart. I guide him to bend over the couch, watching videos of trains on my phone. I rip open the alcohol swab.

What if the pharmacy gave us the wrong stuff?

I pull down his diaper. Then wash his buttocks. Smooth skin. Today the right cheek.

MotherBear5: It's the only thing that's helped.
AutismWarrior: After eight years, my son finally said "mama."

Slow, as if I am conducting music. My hand goes up and down. His skin radiant, alive. I press the alcohol-soaked pad.

Rumor said a doctor once killed an autistic child with alternative treatments. Rumor said a child was healed. The CDC said autism cannot be cured. The New York Times said 10% will "grow out" of it with the right support. A local autism parent told me to avoid all supplements and just accept God. An anonymous neighbor online said autistic children should "be euthanized." A friend of the family said autistic children should be taken into custody if parents use alternative treatments.

I could run this swab over him for hours. He could watch trains for hours. I take off the cap. Needle hovers. Thin as a shred, sharp as a steak knife.

The National Institute of Health conducted a meta-study showing this improves symptoms 30%. The National Institute of Health says this has little to no side effects.

I hold his skin taut. Our pediatric nurse said to aim between 15 and 40 degrees. Sink the needle into his baby fat.

> *Autistic brain cells. Lesions. Atrophy. Studies of dendrites. Recent headline: Brains of Autistic Children Like Alzheimer's Patients.*

Blur. Sofa mealy-colored. The room appears pixelated. His bare cheeks. It's done.

He flinches. Sticky bubbling in his throat rises. Then roars, wail delayed. He pulls his feet, arms, fingers tightly to his body, away from me. Betrayed.

> *I want to collapse. Table with broken legs. I wish he could somehow comfort me, how inappropriate.*

I approach him like a stray, brush the hair around his ears, rest my head on his smooth back and listen to the clashing chug, train wheels along tracks until the video ends.

Nature

All his life, my son has woken
during the night. I've learned
to sleep light, listen

for a creak, thump. He has learned
to unlock the baby-gate
at the top of the stairs.

Yesterday, he showed me
he knows how to unlock the front door:
sliding chain, bolt.

I try to sleep. But cannot.
Coyote season. Dusk and dawn
they traipse across the lawn,

packs hunting for small dogs.
A neighbor saw a small
bear rooting through the trash.

Buy new locks? Research
online. Children with autism
wander. What have other

parents done? Nail windows
shut. Install alarms. "Put a
GPS band on his arm," so

emergency crews can find
the body. One in forty-five
homes like mine

with children
who cannot sleep,
unafraid of the night-steeped

sky. Down the street. Round the block.
Paul Offit, former official
at the CDC, says autism is natural.

Keep sleeping light. Make sure
the lamps burn all night.
This is not natural.

Sad Animals I

Said the Kangaroo, 'I'm ready...
But to balance me well, dear Duck, sit steady...
So away they went with a hop and a bound,
And they hopped the whole world three times round;
And who so happy,—O who,
As the Duck and the Kangaroo?
—*Edward Lear*

I call 311, am transferred to the city's Early Intervention offices. *I need an evaluation for my son.* I am informed all city autism evaluations must occur within 30 days of the call or else our file will be eradicated from the city's computer system.

> Physical Therapist: "I don't see any gross motor problems. Could be he's just lazy?"

> Occupational Therapist: "Sure he has serious problems, but he won't get any services. What do you want me to do?"

One hour, two. Gross motor, fine motor, speech. Psych evals, IQ tests. Different days, different times. The special education specialist takes over three hours—each time you turn your head away, she points her pen tip at you and clucks.

> Eval Q#1: "Are there problems in the family? Between you and your spouse?"

> Eval Q#2: "Any history of drug abuse?"

There's a math, a sanity to the insanity. Each child is evaluated based on five categories. A two-thirds delay in one category, the child will receive services. One-third delay in two or more, a child will receive services. An evaluator shows us a pie.

We receive automated voicemails: "Be available for evaluator between the hours of noon and 5 pm on Saturday." We rush home, our pails unused from the beach. We skip birthday parties. Try to occupy you for hours in the tiny living room of our apartment. We wait for the doorbell all July, Saturdays gone to nothing.

Eval Q#3, to my husband: "Would you say your wife is a cold mother?"

Eval Q#4, to me: "Would you say you coddled your child? Perhaps your attachment suppressed his developmental growth."

They use words like "deficient," "maladaptive." They use computers, iPads, legal pads, broken pencils pulled from grocery bags. They write down everything we say. They write down nothing. They bring intimidating briefcases with tests, timers, electric buzzers. They bring strange dice covered in colors and dots, ask you to roll across our living room rug. They send us a 60-page report filled with real facts mixed with details copied and pasted about other people's children …

> *Child is a two-year old male. Child speaks multiple languages. Child is bilingual in Spanish. Child speaks Russian and will require a special city-funded Russian aide in future classrooms. Child is allergic to peanuts. Child is unwilling to brush teeth. Child has never hugged mother voluntarily.*

I learn to cry on cue to ensure you will get what you need. Learn to gauge my "educated language" for fear of offending the ego of the evaluator. It does not seem to help that I am a licensed therapist.

Your father and I learn to emphasize our concerns. Not your successes. To discuss instances, anecdotes that might-possibly-indicate-who-knows a haphazard chance of something: autism, ADHD, sensory processing, OCD. Because otherwise you would receive nothing—my boy, with lips and heart.

Eval Q#5, "Is he always this emotional?" and writes some thing down when you cry and run to my arms.

Eval Q#6, "Does he ever show any attachment?"

Eval Q#7, "Do you think he would care if you left the room? Are you sure? How do you know?"

You sat there on our rug and heard it all.

Sad Animals II

Draw a sad rabbit you said.

And I did. This is what we used to do. Each night for weeks. Construction paper. Pink, yellow, blue. You would tell me what to draw and what to write, because you did not like the way the marker felt in your hand, pressed to your palm.

Draw a sad elephant. Draw a sad cow. Make him cry.
Draw a sad frog.
Draw a sad squirrel.

Draw a family of sad rabbits. Write "sad rabbit family." No no no, they're sad, they're sad. You cried and demanded when I tried to give an animal a smile. No no no. They're not happy, they're sad.

Ditches

Some mornings the bus is silent. We cannot speak words to each other. We simply cannot speak.

The morning after the landmark study came out "Mortality and Autism Spectrum Disorders," the bus is silent. Gears turning. Pistons muted. We are captured in a metal echo chamber. Heads filled as if underwater. The bus bucks and sways over potholes. Over ditches. Our mothery heads move back and forth in unison. Even the children seem sleepy. Not crying, no laughter.

Just then, another mother turns to stretch. We catch each others' eyes. Just a slip, like a fish swimming past, and in that millisecond, my eyes told her I know. Her son is low functioning, he will likely die before the age of 50, most likely before he graduates from high school. Complications such as kidney disease, respiratory failure, cerebral hemorrhaging. Her eyes told me she knows my son, high functioning. Likely cause of death: suicide.

We are on a bus bringing our sons to preschool. We will likely attend many funerals.

TONY GLOEGGER

Weather

When we walk out the door,
Jesse's respite worker asks him
about the weather. It's February
in Maine and there's snow
on the ground. He answers
"Clouds, wind, too cold."
Still, I have to remind him
to zip his hoodie, ask maybe
we should go back inside,
change his sandals for socks
and boots. He blurts, "No
socks, no shoes" as I dig
my hands deeper into pockets,
trot to the car. His worker
turns down the radio,
shows him his cell phone.
A list of different cities
rolls down the screen,
their current temperatures
next to them. The worker
points to one and Jesse
answers what he'd wear
if he were there, a coat,
or shorts and a tee shirt.
When the worker points
to another, Joshua pauses,
then says, "New York, Tony
house" and I wonder whether
he remembers that eight hour
U Haul drive when he moved
to Brooklyn the summer me
and his mom were in love.

Jesse, five and a half years old,
incessantly sweating and still
marching obsessively room
to room closing every window
tight; sitting on my lap, licking
the burnt orange remnants
of Extra Spicy Doritos off
his fingers as I talk on
the phone; subwaying
to the end of the F line
and jumping Coney Island
waves as it grows too dark
to see, playing *Rosalita,*
We're Having A Party,
A Good Feelin' To Know
on the stereo, blasting them
in the same exact order
anytime his mom called
to say sorry she'd be home
late again from work
as I lift him as high
as the ceiling, bounce
him on the bed over
and over until we both
run out of breath, ready
for a Beach Boys lullaby
to close our eyes, hopefully
help him, me, sleep
through the night, please.

Good

Walking in the neighborhood
Larry twirls like a circus bear
every twenty steps or so, bends
down and pulls up his socks
like Thurman Munson adjusting
his batting gloves before each pitch.
Lee walks down the aisle, sliding
his fingers along the packages
on every shelf, stopping to align
each one perfectly before he keeps
walking. Some kid stares and laughs,
another runs to his mother, eyes
wide with confusion. The mother
smiles at me, her face softens
into an apology and then crumbles,
turns into an *Oh you poor thing*
pitying pose. I look past her, move
closer to Lee, touch his arm, instead
of smacking the nice lady across
her mouth. I hold Robert's hand
as we walk through the park's gate.
He moves like a drunk Pinocchio,
nearly misses the bench as he stops
to sit. Jesse walks down the aisle,
plops down in a window bus seat
smiling widely as cars drive by,
humming his tuneless song, breaking
into loud laughter
                        and I'm five years old
again. Climbing onto the B55 bus
with my leg brace clanking, I drag
my huge booted foot through the crowd
as the people lean against poles,
grab hand grips. An old black woman
gets up, offers her seat to me.
My mom tells me to thank her,
but I whisper, *no thanks*, grab hold
of a pole and hang on, dream
about flying away, disappearing.

At home, I sit on the stoop, watch
some kids play stickball in the street.
A foul ball bounces my way. I catch it,
rub the Pennsie Pinkie as one
of the players runs it down. *"C'mon,
give it back, you retarded gimp."*
I extend my hand. When he gets near,
I tackle him, wrestle him to the ground.
Surprised, he tries to fight back,
struggle out of my hold. I kick him
with my brace. Red pours out of his head.
It felt good. It still feels good.

Magnitude

My friend's wife has a niece
who is autistic. He doesn't seem
to believe that I never wish
Jesse was different. He talks
about missing the big things
like proms and graduations.
I joke about the perks, not
worrying about Jesse driving
drunk on weekends, paying
for college, pretending to like
the woman he wants to marry.
I tell him I take Jesse as he is
and I know what not to expect,
how every new tiny thing
he does grows in magnitude:
the first time he ran to me, grabbed
my hand when I picked him up
at school, the first morning
he walked into our Brooklyn
bedroom to cuddle between us,
that one time he scavenged
through his cluttered sensations,
strung four words together
and told me clearly *"Tony
come back August ."* I explain
I am one of the chosen few
that Jesse invites into his world
and it helps me imagine
I am special with unique super
powers. But yes, I am lying
a bit. I've always wanted to lift
him on my shoulders, six years
old and singing that he believes
in the promised land at a Springsteen
show, play some one on one
in a schoolyard, keeping it
close and never letting him win
until he beat me on his own.
And yes, this past weekend

in Maine, I wish he watched
television. We would have sat
and argued when Girardi
benched A-Rod, ate salty snacks
as the Yanks played the Orioles
in the deciding fifth game.
Instead, I sat on a kitchen stool,
listening to the radio broadcast
while Jesse was happy in his room
tearing pages of picture books
into piles of thin paper strips.

Autistic Basketball

You are following Jesse
through a new-to-you part
of his neighborhood. You ask
if he knows where he's going,
how far, and he says *straight*.
You ask again, he points ahead.
You sat at the morning table
listing activities on the page
he titled Saturday September
15 . He chose basketball instead
of the Lake Champlain ferry.
He walks with his two hands
holding the ball in front of him
like a mechanical waiter
balancing a tray. No dribbling
between his legs, behind his back,
no stutter stepping or head faking,
no flipping it back and forth
between you and him, no racing
across the court, a pass floating
in the air, catching you in stride
as you rise with the memory
of your first taste of schoolyard
grace and lay it softly against
the backboard so the ball settles
in the net's momentary embrace.

Basketball with Jesse means
taking turns for a certain number
of shots. You negotiate, he agrees
reluctantly to 10. You haven't touched
any kind of ball in 7 years: kidney
disease, open heart surgery, hernia
strangulation, dialysis, and finally
the kidney transplant. You get out
of breath trotting a half block
to catch your morning bus, cling
to a pole as it drives, afraid
you'll fall across the aisle

as it turns onto the service
road. You walk slowly, watch
where you step. You stand
at the foul line. Jesse's a step
and a half in front of you.
He's first with a stiff, over
his head, Jack Sikma-like release
that banks it in. You're next, still
trying to imitate Earl The Pearl
of the long gone Baltimore Bullets.
He counts the shots down, only
smiles when he gets to shout
10 so he can go home, sit
at the table, cross basketball
off his list, move on to McKee's
and apple juice with ice, chicken
fingers, French fries, extra hot.
Jesse's 10 for 10, You're 1 for 10
with an air ball. He doesn't care.
You have to tell yourself not to.

Adam Grabowski

Individualized Education Program

Sullivan Elementary School
Holyoke, MA

I.

There's Ms. Marla's room,
heat-thick with the Xerox machine, its hum.
Smell of paint and brown cabinets.
That table, low rectangle and never enough chairs.

Or the conference room, maybe,
window-light cold and wide open.
Six tables rectangled together into one large rectangle,
that huge gulf of space in the middle.
I can see between us, I can see the courtyard.

II.

No one's a hero
in an IEP meeting.

Everyone's trying to save
something—
money
prep time
a job.

This is when
I run into a phone booth
and find I've come out
just a different kind of Clark Kent.

I'm not a poet in
an IEP meeting.

There's nothing to write through,
each moment unseizable.

Though I've tried every bellow in my body.
I can't affect. I can't change.

There's no parent in
an IEP meeting—

not in the behaviorist,
not in the team lead,
not even in me.

More like we're the paddles
in a game of table tennis

and only here
to acknowledge that there's a ball
and movement
and air.

SONIA GREENFIELD

The Lost Boys

It is always telegraphed
when boys are fed
to the elements, so you read
of the one fed first to air
then water from the lip
of a bridge. The one fed
to the fire collected
in the furnace of his
father's sedan. And what
of earth? Old news, the one
searched for with picks
and shovels in the dirt floor
of a basement. I learn
the latest one flung in Oregon
was labeled like mine. In Latin
spectrum means apparition,
and that ghost arcs
from the metal rail over and over
and leaves a trail like a gray
rainbow to the river
below. My own son's
element is water, too.
How he could stand
at the sink and let the wet
feel wash through his fingers
until California is bled dry.
This other boy's mother
must have thought
him cursed by his disorder
or what I call the weird magic
my boy tries to control
and hold in his hands
like a rising lake.

Fukushima Daisies

Half-folded, a cell
half-divided, the center
puckers like lips,

and the white petals
gather like a headdress
on one end, the yellow

not a fleece button,
the petals not a symmetry
of rays. *Fasciation*

is something gone awry
in replication, set apart
from those perfect

blossoms as alike as
school children in tidy
uniforms, yet some

of us see the novel
in what went wrong, some
of us see our one-off

children in those radio-
active flowers clustering
into misfit bouquets.

GEORGE GUIDA

The Other End of the Rope

You are absent from a shot of the hospital façade.
You are lepering behind colonial walls.

The sun is pictorial, glinting off glass
like a warden's flashlight beam in darkened eyes.

The tour shepherds students through
the orphanage infirmary like cosmonauts.

Toddlers are building a family of toys
stuffed solid as forgetfulness.

You sit across the vaulted room from uniforms
who cede them unlit corridors.

A blank-faced boy in harness is also out of frame,
tied with a rope to window bars and sun.

The rope and our shoes share loss-colored dust
with shirtless boys and mangy dogs unraveling the streets.

The other end of the rope is tied to a woman
selling scars at the edge of Shantytown.

The men who plied and blade that pierced her
couldn't sever the binding's pan.

The autistic brain won't read despair in tile squares.
Eyes shine out of focus in the fading shot.

The bound boy hums cleft songs to dying stars,
reciting unseen galaxies.

MAX HEINEGG

Advisory

It's really homeroom. They want
us to call it that—fulfills a state
mandate—a team of fellows came to
our school & saw the students sans
adults tending to their well-
being. We promised to fulfill all
such expectations. In the late 80s,
I feared my teachers as vampires
joking they returned to their wooden
desks that in the moonlight became coffins.
Some terrible suckers must have invited them in.

I saw the chalkboard on the first day of Yearbook:
School sucks, do bongs—the teacher exhaling
poorly feigned shock, purporting
it was scrawled by a burnout.
I know now the hoary head was sad-
laughing his way through merci-
less dust. I've learned to respect
this morning's quintessence: K.'s trusting
stare at me, his barely-brushed hair, asking if
he may get some water. *Why not?*

He asks me what to do about his sore knee.
When I ask where the pain is, he hikes his slacks.
It's around the joint. What should I do?
He's on a plan that one of us doesn't know
the details of. I tell him *Relax,*
we are still before the bell
& that I think he will be alright,
but the nurse should see him.

You see me, right?
Yes, I say, I am looking at you,
& we're talking to each other. Don't worry,
I won't mark you absent.

Quraysh Ali Lansana

echolalia one

language echoing itself.
itself, echoing language
echoing language itself.
language, itself echoing

what i heard them say
say what? them, i heard.
heard them. what i say?
i say what them heard.

i mean these words
these words i mean.
mean these i words.
words mean: these, i.

why don't you hear me?
me you don't hear. why?
hear me, why don't you?
you don't? why? hear me.

you make me angry
angry you make me
make me angry: you
you angry. make me.

in my head i'm not alone.
alone, i'm not in my head.
head, i'm not in my alone
i'm in my head. not alone.

echolalia two

everyday he   reminds
how much more i need
to learn
how smart i am

not
how
i think   i am

smart
don't know
sometimes

if sad
is about

missing mama

or *franny's feet*

flight

I.
ari was in the backseat
of a squad car by the time
i arrived from class, tumblers
painting "the nine" midnight red, blue
red. annoyed butch sista next
door on my stoop, talking how she
could raise my son better, dcfs
already on way. rushing past
i thank her smugly, that she found
him wandering south on evans
mama's weary too deep. two
locks, two flights of stairs & two doors
then wildlife search for lost anaconda
diego and baby jaguar at his heels.
they knew something we lacked.

II.
tired daycare staff said anti-social
not behavior. he plays alone mostly
and enjoys hide and seek, the campus
labyrinth half a football field in size.
no one saw the buddyless boy join
a group walk down the long hall
past administrators and security.
out of door, handholders turn right
ari forward across drive, parking lot
his head lower than hood ornaments.
police spot him near cafeteria, a three
year old undergraduate darting back
to dorm for snack between class. they lose
him in square corridors, endless doors.
twenty minutes later i retrieve message
from office line, cell phone on file, on hip.

III.
gunfire and house arrest family
across street led us across town.
teen sons in age for *what you on
nigga* we found pacific heights in
chicago, playground down the block.
first weekend ari is nocturnal study
new quest, fresh terrain. we are
sprawling search party, hectic moonlight.
four lane, three blocks away, neighbor
spies him at intersection, calls police. bolts
and chains on doors next day too low.
fire escape invites back gate missing
two by four, alley eye open to last night's
corner.

trek

captain, i will go anywhere
you want to go, look both

ways before crossing galaxy
strange world where i lack

the vernacular, you fluent.
rouse me from carbon sleep

with details of mission, coordinates
lurking danger. i will be your

Q, number one, whoever
i must to enlist in this evolving

speculative fiction, magical realism
beyond human reach but not far.

earthlings so non-essential, feign
supremacy. outer space not final.

the spectrum

is a tenuous chaos
a bankrupt ritual
a tedious in-law
an irritable preoccupation
a vapid hoovermatic
a superpower
a kind of grace

golden

> *In life, there's the beginning and the end. The beginning don't matter. The*
> *end don't matter. All that matters is what you do in between—whether*
> *you're prepared to do what it takes to make change.*
>
> John Carlos, 1968 Olympic Bronze Medalist

not mexico city, sunny southside
afternoon. three hundred athletes in neon
tees at football stadium with no lights.

they approach the line, pause and release
softball. lands with pomp & plod, applause
tape measure and clipboard tally distance.

grass unaware of unimaginable feet
i sprint to hug my olympian, trudge
over, around competitors all buzzing

victors this bright and everyday.
ari mounts the podium like everest
giggles when his name is loud

lowers his head, red and blue ribbon
around his neck. gold, no mineral imbalance
here. then right arm, raised fist

in front of maple tree, god & creation
his impulse, unedited verse, truth
and the unexplainable joy in between.

JOANNE LIMBURG

Alice's Walk

If you could feel, as Alice does, how fast the earth is moving

if your bones shuddered at the grinding, forward thrust of it

if you sometimes had to run keep running just to stay in place

if you feared the ground might throw you like a horse its rider

if you knew a foot placed here or there meant life or death

then you wouldn't need to ask her why she walks that way.

Alice Between

Between is stone sometimes;
other times, it's vapour.

It freezes her halfway down
a flight of stairs.

It ripples over the bath
where hot water meets cold air;

when she gets in, she feels it
happening through her.

Sometimes, she is petrified;
sometimes, she sublimes.

Alice's Brother

He sits down on the edge of her college bed, and he says, it's different at home without you. Calmer. The cat's stopped talking, the flowers've shut up too. I know the cards will stay in their pack, chess pieces will wait until I've moved them. I don't have to run to stand still anymore.

You don't know what it's like, having a sister who changes size. When you were small I had to put you in my pocket to keep you safe, and when you were huge, you could fill the whole house. I mean the whole house. It's different without you. There's plenty of room.

Alice's Antism

Ground is home to her, it's where
her gaze can come to rest,

take stock of what has never changed:
the rainbows in the gutter,

the points and circles of the pouring rain,
the pavement's long squared shoulder.

And every summer the ants turn up,
shiny black and perfectly themselves,

bringing out the ant-shaped joy
by which she knows she's Alice still.

The Annotated Alice

Special interests? I loved books, mostly
books with other worlds in them.

When I was three, I would ask my mother
to take *The Annotated Alice* down for me

so I could see the pictures. I was drawn by
that other girl with the unsmiling level look.

She had adventures. My mother told me
how she fell for miles but wasn't hurt,

made friends with a vanishing cat, grew
and shrank and grew, but whatever her size,

stayed curious. She said I was curious too.
I asked a lot of questions. One day, I asked

what would happen if I went through
the looking-glass. Would I go, like Alice,

into another world? No, she said:
I'd wake up in hospital, being mended,

and I was so disappointed. I never meant
to stay forever on the nonsense side.

Ayala Ben Lulu

I'm a Mother

I'm the mother of a pet—
a puppy that wags its tail when it sees you.
But that's not accurate.
Even a dog looks at you and runs to bring you the ball.
Even a dog is happy to play with you.
Maybe like a cat that rubs against your legs when you come into the
house.
But that's not accurate either,
Even a cat snuggles and purrs in your lap.
You are more like a goldfish.
It's pleasant beside you, you're so beautiful, but
you don't even get that I'm here.
I need to try harder.

Translated from Hebrew by Vivian Eden

Aquarium

Like someone born of the sea,
Missing the water's quiet,
Half sea and half land,
That's how we saw you one day,
A two-year-old boy
Inside a large fish tank,
Breathing there quietly.
And we didn't understand how you could.
At first we pulled you out,
But the moment you tried it
You just wanted to go back—
Our love was too loud.

Translated from Hebrew by Vivian Eden

Cyclops

Above your head a moon narrow as a scalpel cut
Peeps pale and soft
Out of the sky's taut skin.

An ambulance wails past.
The neighborhood children in white holiday clothes
Run on the pavement stones.

Milk roams the streets,
Your nipples are swollen.
On your chest you carry in a sling
A baby whose eyes are sealed.
The birthmark on his forehead
Opens at you like an eye
Without a pupil.

Translated from Hebrew by Vivian Eden

SHANE McCRAE

After the Diagnosis

We married in the boy we thought he would

Be honey cinnamon and was the man

A genius   artist mathematician hus-

band father beautiful and is he was

Always so beautiful our son our map

Of us and nobody we knew the sun

A compass in the east   the moon a cres-

cent moon and monsters   dragons barely vis-

ible in the wide sea   near the tall ships

Both on the map and in the world but not

The same monsters on the map and in the world

And not the same   world on the map and in

The world the same sea in the world   and in

The world the monsters stretch from coast to coast

We Married in his Belly

We married in his belly our son's bel-

ly our autistic son we married in

His ghost the son we had   the son we have

His ghost we didn't know him in his bel-

ly no   we did not know him not the son

We had we do not know the son we have

We've read about him sometimes in the books

The Have-You-Seen-This-Child books all night we

Read all night searching for our son   but dai-

ly parts of the son we have disintegrate

And disappear   we don't know who we're look-

ing for we married in his belly   we

Would know it if we saw it now no way

To see it now no way to see inside

He Turns a Corner

And we divorced in every time my heart / He turns a corner stops   he turns

And I can't see him anymore   / And he

autistic children run away / And he

I pick him up from school he runs

Out of the room ahead of me   and down the hall

I pick him up from day care   but we call it school   / And he

will never be with kids like this again

Kids who aren't like him

And every time he runs   ahead of me away   / And down the hall

to the corner and

around / The corner

and he disappears

Ahead of me and I can't make him

stop   or turn / Runs

laughing through the door   into the dark

We Married in the Front Yard

We married in the front yard watch-

ing our son disappear   our two-year-old

Son Nicholas we watched him disappear

Gesture by gesture   word by word his au-

tism slowly   erasing him he couldn't catch

A ball   he could have caught the ball before

Forgot   the word for ball we didn't know

Which mattered more   the action or the word

Which disappearing part was more   impor-

tant more   our son which part   to hold and which

Part to let go we said the word and rolled

The ball again we said   the word and rolled

The ball we rolled the ball and we said   catch

He held his arms out   and embraced the air

MEGAN MERCHANT

Cradling an Empty Cup

The neurologist says
absence seizures,
so I add a drop of water.

The therapist says
drool, and I take a sip—
we have already prepared

for this slippery season
by covering our hands
in rubber gloves.

She says no, we must
persist, long-road,
think ahead.

I add two.

Then *spectrum, expressive delay,
attention deficit,*

the jaw lock, mid-coke
and tears so silent that when
I moved to check his face,

(hearing that long
train whistle of instinct)

I found him,
a mime performing pain.

Eight drops.

Hands flapping like wings
trying to catch the
splint of sun,

one.

Gull-mouth
cradling
salt-rusted words,

two.

I carry the cup
while driving,
wandering alone
through the store,

folding laundry into paper cranes,
borrowing the words for this poem,

I carry the quiet-stub of sorrow,

add a drop when each
wired word
disconnects
and

his stations fuzz.

Day-by-day, the cup
grows heavier, my arm aches

deep in the bone,

not because of the balance,
or weight —

a drop or two different—

but because I'm refusing
to set it down.

A witness' job is not to cure,
but carry,

so I sing the first bars of each lullaby,
and tuck a white sheet,
a half-moon
embrace,

staying awake
in case he rises and shapes

his empty hands
into the sign for water.

KAMILAH AISHA MOON

Love is a Basic Science

They ran tests.
Looked for reasons
she learned like molasses.

She didn't like to be touched.
Walked on her tiptoes
everywhere, a braided
ballerina in flip-flops or Keds.
Our way of walking
a plodding, ill-fitting gait
that continued to confound.

It wasn't extraordinary in our minds
to love her,
to let her know,
holding on until she squeezed back.

Achilles Tendon: War at 3 PM

Playground henchmen trailed me,
nipped at my heel.

Nerf-ball taunts whizzed
by my ear. I headed toward dinner
and being tucked in—away
from jellybean rivalries
that wouldn't mean much
once we traded arithmetic for algebra,
wiped salty words
off my brow.
Until a few yards later,
YOUR LITTLE SISTER IS A RETARD
sliced me.

I went down fighting.
Took them with me
in a hail of fist-fire.

Except I rose.
Her honor saved,
gauze and hydrogen peroxide fizzing
in broken skin.

(Middle Sister)

For most of elementary school,
people thought we were twins.
At a glance, she "passed"
next to me.

Linger; we become distinct.

My eyes sparkled green.
I had words, my mind mostly in a world
I made up long before I knew why
I needed my own.

Her eyes shimmered brown.
She made random noises
that reminded me of TV static,
shook her head "No" at questions
I couldn't hear.

I was mad when she arrived.

But I got over it soon enough
and began to get it, began to bare
my new teeth at those
who ignored my near-twin.

Memory in the Park

Swinging was the closest thing
to flying then. Pushing off
a little harder each time, we sailed
above the monkey bars
and the first tier of maple limbs.

I remember the day when she swung
back and forth unattended—beaming
as giggles rode the wind shotgun with her.

I saw her pleasure naked.
I saw it.

No Room for Gray

Between is a hard place to live.

She shuns wheelchairs and
mongoloid faces, mad that her mind
will fight to keep her
quarantined
from her own car, yard,
babies.

You are. Or you are not.
You're sick. Or you're well.
One thing. Or another.
But it's never that simple
like breathing should be.

Between is a hard place to live.

Each morning she stretches
her fingers toward a life
just out of reach,
and grudgingly squeezes
into a seat at a table
that bumps her knees.

Directions

Don't drop your sister. Ever.
Especially when I'm gone. I don't believe
you care as much as I do. I want to, but
how could you, really?

And should you? Gorgeous wind
in your sails. But I need you
to carry her, to want to carry her.

Hold her hands on both sides, crossings ahead
swift and brutal. Never let her out of your sight,
like years ago in the park, in the mall, at the movies.
Like after church on the lawn when your father
wasn't looking, didn't correct those who only asked
about the first two. Promise me she won't inhale
the ammonia smell of group mess halls,
wince at the prying fingers of hired help.

Promise me, girls.

OLIVER DE LA PAZ

Autism Screening Questionnaire—Speech and Language Delay

1. Did your child lose acquired speech?

A fount and then silence. A none. An ellipse
between—his breath through
the seams of our windows. Whistle
of days. Impossible bowl of a mouth—
the open cupboard, vowels
rounded up and swept under the rug.

2. Does your child produce unusual noises or infantile squeals?

He'd coo and we'd coo back. The sound
passed back and forth between us like a ball.
Or later, an astral voice. Some vibrato
under the surface of us. The burst upon—
burn of strings rubbed
in a flourish. His exhausted face.

3. Is your child's voice louder than required?

In an enclosure or a cave it is difficult to gauge
one's volume. The proscenium of the world.
All the rooms we speak of are dark places. Because
he cannot see his mouth, he cannot imagine
the sound that comes out.

4. Does your child speak frequent gibberish or jargon?

To my ears it is a language. Every sound
a system: the sound for dog or boy. The moan
in his throat for water—that of a man with thirst.
The dilapidated ladder that makes a sentence
a sentence. This plosive is a verb. This liquid
a want. We make symbols of his noise.

5. Does your child have difficulty understanding basic things ("just can't get it")?

Against the backdrop of the tree he looks so small.

6. Does your child pull you around when he wants something?

By the sleeve. By the shirttail. His light touch
hopscotching against my skin like sparrows.
An insistence muscled and muscled again.

7. Does your child have difficulty expressing his needs or desires using gestures?

Red faced in the kitchen and in the bedroom
and the yellow light touches his eyes
which are open but not there. His eyes
rest in their narrow boat dream and the canals
are wide dividing this side from this side.

8. Is there no spontaneous initiation of speech or communication from your child?

When called he eases out of his body.
His god is not our words nor is it
the words from his lips. It is entirely body.
So when he comes to us and looks we know
there are beyond us impossible cylinders
where meaning lives.

9. Does your child repeat heard words, parts of words, or TV commercials?

The mind circles the mind in the arena, far in—far in
where the consonants touch and where the round
chorus flaunts its iambs in a metronomic trot. Humming
to himself in warm and jugular songs.

10. Does your child use repetitive language (same word or phrase over and over)?

A pocket in his brain worries its ball of lint.
A word clicks into its groove and stammers
along its track, Dopplering like a car with its windows
rolled down and the one top hit of the summer
angles its way into his brain.

11. Does your child have difficulty sustaining a conversation?

We could be anywhere, then the navel of the red moon
drops its fruit. His world. This stained world drips its honey
into our mouths. Our words stolen from his malingering afternoon.

12. Does your child use monotonous speech or wrong pausing?

When the air is true and simple, we can watch him tremble
for an hour, plucking his meaning from a handful of utterances
and then ascend into the terrible partition of speech.

13. Does your child speak the same to kids, adults, or objects (can't differentiate)?

Because a reference needs a frame: we are mother and father
and child with a world of time to be understood. The car radio
plays its one song. The song, therefore, is important.
It must be intoned at a rigorous time. Because rigor
is important and because the self insists on constant vigils.

14. Does your child use language inappropriately (wrong words or phrases)?

Always, and he insists on the incorrect forms.
The wrong word takes every form for love—
the good tree leans into the pond,
the gray dog's ribs show, the memory
bound to the window, and the promise of the radio
playing its song on the hour. Every wrong form
is a form which represents us in our losses,
if it takes us another world to understand.

Autism Screening Questionnaire: Abnormal Symbolic or Imaginative Play

1. Does your child flap his hands or other finer flapping? Does he self stimulate?

In ecstatic moments, a kind of remembering
the body is the body. For example, these are arms
for grasping. These hands are for
holding and touching the known and unknown.
And how remarkable it all is—scintillate the way
wonder surges towards the filaments.

2. Does he bang his head?

On the inside, the retort of feeling accumulates
as weight. It is like smoke had risen
to the cellar and suddenly became thick and resinous.
A song heard while submerged in a pool.

3. Does he self mutilate? Inflict pain or injury?

Huddled close against the thrum of rainfall
on our roof and his fingers hook
into my eye-sockets. It is always
this: his fingers seek emptiness to fill, chorus
of nails pressed into my flesh thrust into the seam
of our borders. My body. His pain. Our pain.

4. Does he toe walk? Possess clumsy body posture?

Foal-sure and big-footed he tumbles
across the laminate. Shaky
flicker of sense up the spinal pathways.
Synaptic leaps saying
move or glide. The effort of nerves
to shape the body's urgencies
stuttering into what's stuck.

5. Does he arrange toys in rows?

Because design is a prism of the mind.
Because placement is in relation to.
Because the polyglot of form needs order.
Because blue car next to green car
next to red car all along the highway.
Because the serpentine of die cast metal
relentlessly gleams. Because form
is relentless, relentlessly infinite.

6. Does he smell, bang, lick, or inappropriately use toys?

Unbuffered tang. Metallic with a murmur
of salt. An ersatz flavor fevering plastics.
Having tasted sugar. Having known
sugar when knowing is a haunt.
A shape in the mouth that is not a soufflé
and not a seed. This palpable fat.
This gummy warmth.
This tender unknown.

7. Does he focus interest on toy parts such as car wheels?

Every object has a purpose. Every purpose hums its will.
Plastic tires in close orbits. Firestones nearly spun
into the eye. As if the urge to become the eye
was the tire's concern. The idea that the thing
could move beyond the membranes
of the self to become fully boy. To be sewn into
the boy's mind. And having been possessed, intensely
by the thing, upon the thing's cessation, grief.

8. Is he obsessed with objects or topics?

The *Amanita* genus is his favorite and includes the "death cap."
You will know a death cap by its off-colored patches,
the remnants of what was once a veil that had surrounded
the mushroom when it was young. We had lived
in a place of quiet, surrounded by every manner of fungus
and he would stand in the rain until drenched looking
at the same clump of mushrooms. Fairy rings. Polypore shelves.
Sleek and concealed little spore bearers hidden under leaves.
Lobes of chanterelles. The coral-like hemispheres of morels
thinking in their darkness.

9. Does he spin objects, himself? Is he fascinated with spinning objects?

Pinwheels staked along the sidewalk.
Their abiding gyres a mess of colors. He seems
to take them as evidence of
the refuge. An embrace behind the eyes.
A wild ecstasy trammeled by a center. It hones him in.
His being wound down as one winds a clock to take
ample measure of what is infinitesimally
daunting and thus pulled in by the swirl.

10. Are his interests restricted? (Does he watch the same video over and over?)

In the dark. In the night. In the glow of the day. Audible fuzz
of the screen like passing rain. Shuddering spray of TV light.
Its pixelated filaments pierce the gloom, splits the gap that veils
in from out. The image makes a testament constantly upheld.

11. Does he have difficulty stopping a repetitive "boring" activity or conversation?

The toy truck's wheels rotate clockwise then counter.
In the sand box he puts his eyes close to the wheels, the sand
hisses out from the treads and into the tender folds
of his eye, its membranes soft tissues. The pain
must be unbearable and still he pushes me away as I try
to reclaim him from whatever mystery holds him. From whatever
far away place whistles to his brain—its boulevard of wheels
spinning past his bewildered imagination.

12. Does he have an unusual attachment to objects—sticks, stones, strings, hair, etc.?

Pocketful of stone: chalcedony and pyrite. The milky ghost
of quartz. Tiger's eye. Iron flakes wedged into thin veins.
Ores reluctantly peering in tentacle-like threads, sewn into
igneous rhyolite. Peppered granites and rounded skipping stones
palmed and warm. He'd demand I carry them all in my pockets.
All of their weight pressed against my thigh, raucous with each step.

13. Is he stubborn about rituals and routines? Is he resistant to change?

Head down, his mind a needle. Intellect extended into
the tip where his concentration pierces the veil. A thousand
tiny exit wounds of time against the backdrop of the sun
becomes a galaxy. A galaxy of pin pricks where the seasons
never change and October is always October, the forms
of constellations immutable. Never ebbing. Never
unreliably winking out like gods of firm promises.

14. Are his tastes restricted by consistency, shape or form?

His mouth cradles the form that is most consistent with a memory.

15. Does he have a savant ability or a restricted skill superior to his age group?

His mind teems with magical thought—
the possibilities of every moment: if the clock were a cicada
winding down; if the rain were an unfurled scroll of lost voices;
if the sky held all the animals everyone had loved, then
the absolutes holding us here with our grief are not sovereign.
That this alchemy, scratched with debris and errata, these waves
sweeping our houses loose from their pilings, all of it is soluble
in the swirling cacophony of the mind.

Autism Screening Questionnaire: Social Interaction Difficulties

1. Does your child have poor eye contact? Does he stare from unusual angles?

Yes. Like a dark bird from a high perch.
Yes. With acetylene torches lit somewhere in the distance.
    With eyes wide as the Morpho's iridescence.
Yes. Wild and hot like fixed stars.

2. Does your child not seem to listen when spoken to directly?

We call it dappled thoughts. He is constantly dappled—
here and not here. He is a thrush hidden in the sage.

3. Does your child have excessive fear of noises? Does he cover his ears frequently?

With wind there are moments—agonies. Like the time
we found him covering his ears in a cement sewer pipe
during a storm or when he fled into the street, shocked
by the vacuum. Often we hold him hard to keep the world
from flooding in. Often the world is sirens.

4. Does your child seem like he is in his own world?

We mourn him daily. And yet he guides me by the hand
through the threshold of his room as one guiding someone
just off a train, gently and lightly, avoiding the gap between
the platform and the track. The heat from his hand,
combustion-warm. Old stove in which we've heated this house.

5. Does he lack curiosity about his environment?

Because the color of the red door renders it mute.
Because the color of the die-cast car is an empty blue
and the sound of our voices could be any possible starling
we are not here. He is not here. And what of the place you reside
if you don't reside in it? Where then does your body blink?

6. Do his facial expressions not fit situations?

Nulled into a thick disquiet. Mouth agape.
Agate of the eye catches quick the inseam and
no blemish. No, no turning away and no smile.
The contraption shuts its winking gap.

7. Does he cry inappropriately? Does he laugh inappropriately?

A soothing so honed it does not surface
or salvage the daily losses. Which are also sharp
vibratos of hums along the jawbone—the music's
arrowing shot into the thalamus. A strobe's command
and call. A conspiratorial ache.

8. Does he have temper tantrums? Does he overreact when he doesn't get his way?

He is a dark and stabled bull kicking at the chained gate.

9. Does he ignore pain? For example, when he bumps his head, does he react?

If it strikes you can't rescind it. Juncture to
the brain. Sharp cortical hurt into which
leap charges—synapse to synapse, but then a what?
A question asks its question. A hurt insists and yet.

10. Does he dislike touch? Doesn't want to be held?

There's something about proximity. The dutiful
belonging of atoms and how we relate
the world through our skin. The exposed parts
of ourselves and how those pavilions are brushed by
a plum tree's wicked thorns.

11. Does he hate crowds? Does he have difficulties in restaurants and supermarkets?

Everyday he's praying through the meanwhiles.
The sequences of. Not just aflutter, but alone
he sits on the periphery. Ears beside his little body.

12. Is he inappropriately anxious? Scared?

To soothe, the sound of humming through teeth. And so
a symphony of fears. The ventricular outbursts pleat
the clouds. The sky is always exploding
and in that delirum, a curdled tone.

13. Does he speak the same to kids, adults, or objects?

Remind us of our asymmetries. Who is that again? And what
smile to let the darkness in? I see him speak to the man
in blue work clothes and the way his face yields to
the light. To the way moments like this explode.

14. Does he use language inappropriately? (Wrong words or phrases).

The world is a network of minds. Think
of the tongue and the fibers that make
its muscles. The branching capillary network
enmeshed. Alive and cooled with a song
that slides away. Tongue jammed in its stirrup
thinking of itself and the blood red
amanitas pushed out of the earth.

JOEL DIAS PORTER

Portrait of the Artist as a Starfish in Coffee

What if the primary colors on your spectrum
were mud, muddle and muddiest?
Benjamin Franklin invented the Internet
so that we could talk to folk but not face to face
and I know what purple-tailed hawk of thought
just perched on the top bones of your extended wrist
but try to see your average feet in my size 17s,
Fact: The average reader processes 300 wpm
and maybe you can read other people's faces
like a vegan interrogating a list of ingredients
but what if every face was written in Braille
and you had only catcher's mitts below your wrists,
or IKEA bookcases with reams of instructions
ciphered in micro print with disappearing ink,
and imagine being so literal that when told
to let sleeping dogs lie, you asked
how a Doberman could be dishonest
or imagine having only the emotional scope
of a toddler's eight box of crayons, or so deaf
to subtext that every smiling hint a girl ever sent
was in a prescription bottle with a You-proof cap
or a personal pizza delivered hours late
to the door of a boarded up summer bungalow
then try to out-do that dose of pepperoni
with scandal-sized scoops of organic skew,
Fact: The U.S. has over 95,000 miles of shoreline,
but on this dinner plate the border between the Country
of carrots and the Province of peas could never meet,
Say your brain is a slinky Bullet headed train
but your mouth is a horse drawn Amish wagon
and what rockets across the endless gray rails
of your origamied cranium is ever projected
onto your grinning scrim of skin,
and maybe Ben Franklin didn't
invent the Internet, but the Internet does

contain pictures of him inventing electricity
which in theory is the same thing,
say your friend Gigi claims it might storm later
and you maybe hear Oran Juice Jones singing
"I saw you (and him) walking in the rain"
and you beam a lighthouse smile,
only Gigi says "Seriously I saw it on the news"
while somehow all you smell is full length fur coats
matted by a downpour in MacArthur Park and
now Gigi wants to know what's so funny
but who could say Oran Juice Jones
without a concentrated face so you try
to collect the loose nickels and pennies
of thought spilling from your front pocket
but Gigi fires up her smartphone
to show you the seven day forecast
and now the foil covered pots on the back
of her electric range are beginning to boil
and you say "No, I believe you"
but she believes in tone of voice the way Crayola
once believed in a peach crayon called "Flesh"
or the way some banks only vouch for daily deposits
left by a river's most assiduous visits,
Fact: The City of Pittsburgh has over 400 bridges,
most of which do not cross rivers, but
let's say you arch quick when softly pricked as
if any foreign finger were a cattle prod
and maybe Ben Franklin didn't invent electricity
but he certainly earned a shiny penny by cutting
out the lights during thunderstorms, only your steady tone
might as well be a mono Sinatra single
on the platter of a hand cranked Victrola,
as Gigi cocks her head like a small dog
peering into the conch-like roar of a horn
and your hopes seem like the five branches
of an invertebrate drying on a bean colored beach
when she steams to a Java Sea beyond
the spectrum of any radial arm's spiny reach.

Annual Meeting in April

it's on a Wednesday this time
and I'm prepared for all
of the same discussions

your caseworker and
group home leader,
your sister and I, meet in a small room
with chairs that hurt my back

yes, you still need help
getting dressed,
and no you still
don't talk.
you'd think by age 32
they would stop asking

yes you are making progress,
and staying close to your group
on long walks

yes, you still come home
every Sunday afternoon

the program manager's hands
are a flurry of notes and page turning

I watch you across the room
rocking silently
and your half smile
becomes the whole of me

I hold your hand
on the way out to the parking lot
you kiss my forehead
then, I stand on my tip toes
to kiss you back

I used to think autism
was a war I was fighting
but now, I've taken up residence
in the small village outside of the
battle zone
and spend long days
beneath a cathedral of quiet trees

Sunday Afternoon home visit

I put a blanket over your lap
you need the weight of it
to calm

you flap your hands anyway
a flutter beneath the warm

you tell me you are thirsty
not with words
but with that familiar push
on my right shoulder

you've spilled the cup of water
I brought you
I get up,
walk past the book shelf
with the alphabetical line
of autism books
and I realize not one
has taught me
how to hold this loss

I anguish about your life
after I'm gone
I wonder what your sister
will say to you

I wonder if you think of me
at night

I look across the room
and realize the all the answers
are in your hands

Annual Review

We gather in a small room
tables, chairs
half filled notebooks that try to tell your story

Someone new assigned to your case
asks me questions
I have answered a thousand times

No he can't brush his teeth
No he can't make his own meals
Yes he tries to make his bed
sometimes he buses his own plates

sometimes he cries
we don't know why
sometimes he tears his clothes to shreds
—then we buy new ones

One hour and twenty minutes pass
each person at the table
closes their files

I want to tell them
how you said "cheese" once
when you stood at the refrigerator

back then
there were no case managers
no funds to be disbursed
no team meetings

just a boy
whose blond hair I combed each morning

and a silence
that knew which way
we were headed

You are Twenty-Three Years Old

People have stopped sending us the
"miracle cure for autism" articles

friends at parties have stopped asking
"will he grow out of it ?"

the science reports
climb out of the radio each day
genetics
environmental assaults
what's in the water
but nobody really knows

I keep my words sparse
so people can go on
worry about their own lives
parents in nursing homes
kids in college

the group home is closer now
you are home every weekend
I watch your sister learn to care for you
her tone of voice has changed
is tinged with mothering

I watch her hands learn to
fold things
napkins, your clothes,
unspoken needs

I step out of the living room sometimes
know you will be okay for a few minutes

unfold the mail carefully
sort things into stacks
that make sense

I'll be starting dinner soon
and although you've never told me
I know how much you love
the chicken I will make

you and I both know
how it must simmer
for the longest time

A Hero Twelve Miles Away

to Tom's group home provider Orlando

It's not because
every day you make sure
six young men are dressed and bathed
—ready for another day

It's not because you make sure
they all go to the dentist and get check-ups
or that you drive them to Fisherman's Wharf
on Saturday afternoons

It's because in the morning
you straighten my son's clothing
as if it were your own

It's because just before I shut the door
I watch my son wrap his hands
around the crook of your elbow
and I know he will be okay
even after the sun has left me
and the house has gone dark

It's because I thought
I would never go to Disneyland
with my son again
but you drove for eleven hours
in a van with six disabled young men
and four staff members
and let me go quietly
on the Peter Pan ride when everyone was hungry
for dinner

It's because now when I drive up the street
and park in the driveway
I will find you spackling a damaged wall
or tending to the sprinkler in the front yard
perfecting the art of fixing what's broken

I remember the first night
when I had to leave my son with you
and how you let me call
as many times as I needed

I didn't know what he would be having
for breakfast the next morning
I didn't know what pajamas
you would choose for him to wear that night

but I knew that somehow
the twilight would know
and I could trust you
to see the complexities of its shadows

Sometimes at night when it's late
and the last lamp is shut off in the house
I think back to the first loss
how a diagnosis can sever the limbs of knowledge

how the phrase "group home"
can make the walls crumble

I think about how different a road feels
when you drive *to* something
as opposed to *away*

and then I think of you
and I think about my son
sleeping in his room twelve miles away
—how a life can be wrapped
and unwrapped in a thousand different colors

how one person
can make an origami out of
any shape of loss
and make it somehow
feel like gratitude

Non-Verbal

People often ask
"since he can't speak.....
"how do you know what he wants?"

which is often followed
with a moment of my own silence

how do I know when it's dawn

how do I know when the fog
rises up over the eastern hill

how do I know
when Orion is stretched out
across the Autumn sky

I hear your footsteps
as you come downstairs
before I am out of bed
on Sunday morning

each measured footstep
like a far away drum beat
I have become accustomed to
in a dense forest
of silent blooms

Cure

News headlines fill the papers
genetic links
possible breakthroughs closer
another article folded
and placed in the bottom
of my purse

I wonder if the next generation
might be spared

I wonder what other lives
will be folded
into these measured spaces

I don't know what scientist
will see the answer through
a microscope I will never touch

but all too often
I think about a mother
who hears the sound
of her young son tapping
tapping, tapping
the headboard
in the middle of the night

Charlie, A Boy in My Son's Group Home

One Sunday a month
I would make the same trip
the ending always filled with good byes
—layered regret

each time before I left for the long trip home
I walked across the room
to find you
in your same chair
staring into space
as if the blank air knew some way to
apologize for the life you had

your eyes fixed, far away

I approached
held my hand flat open
and you would take hold of it

your young, textured skin spoke to me
in its silence
told me you knew
your family hadn't visited you
in six years

how empty the cove
of a palm can seem

I often ponder those moments now
six months have passed
since we moved our son closer to home

but I can't stop thinking of you
still looking far away
hands folded
as the afternoon
falls on itself
trying to find forgiveness
for having left the morning
too soon

CELESTE HELENE SCHANTZ

The Disappointed Women

These are the tssking women;
the women who glance sideways at my son.
These are whispering women,
who talk behind their hands;
who wait for the bus with their precious brats,
little rats with normal brains,
mimicking my boy as he talks
to the wind, to the robins;
speaks in signs with small fingers
flying fast as hummingbird wings. He tries
to join their circle, flaps and smiles; they move away.
We'll attend another sort of school today;
at this ugly curb; the bus diesel and pesticide
mist the petalled morning. This is the classroom;
this is where we learn a perfect hate.
It blooms and snakes beneath our well-groomed lawns—
the light and shadows arranged, fancy as the sympathy bouquet
you hold out to every mother of a unicorn child.
We choose to hate among these flowers.
I've finally learned to deadhead this pain you offer;
but at 40 it was all unbearable.
At 40 I tried to run away.

At 40, dear neighbor,
I was an old woman who wanted to die.

Just Work

Don't look up. Go shovel.
If you don't do it, someone else will,
and they'll do it for less.
Unload every crate, alone.
Cut your pallet cords one at a time and unload.
Get out mops, sponges, the bucket;
scrub the rusted ring in the men's urinal
with Bon Ami. Gas yourself
with Green Machine and Clorox fumes
'till you can't see straight. It's nothing, you know.

You've worked three, four jobs at a whack
but you're still on the dole.
You've stood frozen stiff at the trains
while the boxcars earthquake past;
stood frozen stiff at the bus stop;
taken the number seventeen
to your old house on Garfield Street;
goose-stepped up that icy unplowed driveway;
your kid's standing at the door letting the heat out,
says what took you so long
and there's a box with cheese sauce
on the counter, 'just add beef."
I say we've got no beef, cheese will do.
Frozen peas, 99 cents.
It all boils over on the stove.

Your kid says please play the game with me—

the one with the pillows
and the castle at the end.
And you could just cry. So just cry.

You could nod off at the bath,
babbling with the faucet
about the beautiful bright tomorrows,
that old woman whispering *hush.*
Maybe if you look hard,
there's still just a glimpse of something good
past the corner of this late December night.

You can almost make out your ancestors
watching you beyond the streetlamp;
you think they're watching you,
saying come on now—
you can do it.
So you do it.

Because even though the rafters
are falling down around you,
even though the welfare ghosts bang their heads
against your walls and hang themselves
in your closet door at three a.m.,
just work.
You'll do it because this kid isn't any kid.
He's your kid.
For him, you did it today.
And you'll do it tomorrow
You just work.

Tomorrow comes early.
All the boozed-up lost souls dancing on bone piles
in the slums of this Golgotha—
they'll all still be there.

But for tonight, for now, you sink
into the blue of the ancient night, you sleep…
a weighted stone or like an amphora sinking
from a burning ship, you just set yourself adrift.
Drift in and out of dreams, be free; a vessel
in the buoyant tide; elusive, sometimes resting,

but don't you dare ever say you're lost.

The Observation Room

"Please sit in our circle on the mat. You may sit on a yellow circle a blue square or a red triangle; those are your choices. Please sit, keep your feet tucked under you."

The story lady has a fringed scarf knotted in a fashionable way. I watch her from a secret room behind the one-way observation glass. Evan stands over by the classroom window, alone. He's not focused on story time or on the pretty teacher. He doesn't speak. His expression is blank. Often, he won't look you straight in the eye. This is called 'lack of affect' in the pamphlet from the doctor's office. Outside, tree boughs rustle in the wind.

The story lady frowns. "Is Evan sitting in the circle?" she says. "No. he's standing at the window looking at nothing. Why are you standing there? You're staring out at the morning but it's time for story. Evan!" She uses a new, sweet voice, sticky as a box of apple juice. The other children listen in their cute outfits; princesses, trucks; they sit cross-legged and hands on lap, silent, compliant, smiling in the Venn diagram of carpet, circle, apple and normal.

The pretty teacher gets up and walks over to him. She tries to guide him back to the mat. "It's time to focus." Evan pulls away, growls and turns back to the window and points and smiles. "I'm sorry," she says, "I have no idea what you're showing me." He reaches for her hand but she goes back and sits down with the others. He's an extremely handsome little boy. She looks over at me behind the observation window. "See? This is the defiant behavior I'm talking about." She's speaking to me, the faceless mother-in-the-wall. The other children's heads turn to search out the nothing space behind the mirror wall she is talking to. I look at Evan. He looks out the window. "Teacher says, if you're not a good boy, no recess. It is time to learn about colors and shapes and then we will sing a happy song." Finally, she shrugs and reads her story to the group.

Evan and I are looking out of our windows. My hand covers my mouth as though I am silencing myself. *"May I please be excused?"* I want to scream. *"May I be excused from this dark hidden room behind a wall?"* I get up to leave. As I pass the class doorway I whisper to the teacher "Thanks. I'll call you this afternoon!" I smile, sounding confident, reassuring. The teacher nods without looking up. From down the hall I can hear the children cheerfully answer her questions in unison. Evan's voice is not there. He's lost in glass, bird and tree, wild sky.

Moments later, outside, I see him framed by the window above. The school was built at the turn of the century. It's very sturdy, lovely brick. He waves through his reflection; I cross the muddy school grounds, inhaling fresh April air and fragrant earth. I'm able to breathe. Now the sun comes out. My son's small hand presses the pane over my head. He tries to touch me. I wave. This hour is gentle and full of promise. The season is as beautiful and unbearable as the heart.

Parked school bus reflects this sun
one raucous flower
in an asphalt field

ANGELINE SCHELLENBERG

What Doctors Took Seven Years to Discover

He sits cross-legged on the sofa.

In his lap, a library book about Amazing Alphie,

a little computer wired

differently from all the others. Yelled at.

Laughed at. Saves the day.

A tear slides down my boy's lip,

but his eyes are calm. *I'm Alphie,* he says.

Relieved this feeling finally has a name.

Support Group 1

We stare at sample schedules and fill the margins with doodles of exploding houses.

We hold up stories like broken playthings: the school that ordered Medicated Barbie, the Child and Family Services G.I. Joe.

We finger a rosary of failures in our pockets.

The fluorescent light carries a tune we've learned to hum.

We clutch bags filled with earplugs and smooth stones.

We wait for someone to bring up Prozac and slide to the edge of common sense.

We gnaw the insides of our cheeks.

We play one-downmanship games for tokens of pity:

> Children who may never say *I love you,*
> Teens able to say *I want to die,*
> Bolters before tires that won't stop squealing in our sleep.

We wear our disillusionments like cloaking devices.

We don't make eye contact.

What I Told the School Division Bigwig in My Head after the Meeting

He's not deaf. He hears

everything you

see—fluorescent lights exciting

mercury vapor in a high-intensity

reaction, the classroom door as it screams

open, the teacher's soles on cold

tile, the wall clock counting

down the seconds till she

notices his pen not

moving. Her breath

on his neck.

The Imaginative Child Gets a Dog

You can tell a Shepadoodle
from a Labradinger, you pore over pictures
of spays and sutures, you can rate
the heat tolerance of any terrier or hound,
but you won't stop
feeding Lily chocolate chips
under the table to see how long
till she pukes. You say *weird,*
weird, this shepherd-corgi cross
who snubs fruits and veggies,
won't bark or fetch—you suspect
Aspergers. Your brand of torture has
a vaudeville touch: paws shoved into pirate coats,
tutus, and kilts; Lily's brown eyes
beneath your Minnie Mouse ears begging me
for rescue. You hide your head under the covers
when her tongue calls you to breakfast,
push away her kiss goodnight,
but here you are, three a.m., wedged
behind the kennel, fingers laced
between the bars, reaching
for her ear.

What Happened after He Colored Outside the Line

A scream.

He's up.

Don't touch!

I run behind him,

around the sanctuary,

chase him into the basement

class, far from street

exits and frightened ushers and hushed

prayers, I block the door with both arms, scan

for pens, scissors, free-standing shelves, anything

glass, I breathe,

I begin to speak slowly, softly, everything I know

about hovercrafts:

how they float

on a cushion of trapped

air, how they have less footprint

pressure than a one-legged seagull,

how we will build one with a leaf

blower in the garage, how they rescue

people from thin ice and

flood, until he hears and falls to the floor, trembling,

lets me squeeze his shoulders,

stroke his damp hair, until he looks in my eyes

and wants to know: *Why is the chair upside down?*

Why is your arm red?

Support Group 3

Oh my God oh my God oh my God! Tracy's mom flaps her hands over
our donuts like a priest on speed because she R-R-Rolled Up the
Rim to Win a coffee, beside Brady's mom who doesn't look up from
picking her peeling cuticles and staring at the crystal lamp she
lost on eBay—*the one that sparkled!*—while Cody's mom grimaces at
Katie's mom and her looping story of the dog that's been missing
since 1982. From the screaming orange walls, *Hit me baby one more
time!* jabs my ribs apart and I curl up inside like a night crawler in
a sunbeam. We know every line in *Pride and Prejudice.* We collect
Bazinga! shirts and badass bows. We laugh at farts and cry at yard
sales. We agree our kids take after their silent fathers. We steer clear
of crowds and wool.

Anything Besides

I will write about something—anything—besides
this

because my heart can't take
one more child blistering in shitty pants
because schools are busy teaching other children to
count,

one more breaking
story about a child wandering off
to drown in a ditch
fifty feet from home.

I can't spend one more moment on regret
over the expert advice I should have ignored
the nights I wept outside your door
as I held it shut,

one more moment of rage
over everything they shouldn't have said:
But he looks so normal. She just needs a good
spanking. Have you tried
enemas? I don't know
how you do it.

It—by which they mean
get out of bed. As if
they haven't considered
the alternative.

I won't repeat
how tired I am of hearing
that vegan cheese will
change everything.

ALISON STONE

Asperger's

As a girl I was awed by his ease
with algebra and actors' birthdays. Sage
of monster trivia, pariah among peers
who pushed him and tore pages
from his books. Terrified, I sucked grape
popsicles beside him on the grease-
stained couch as families fled Rodan's grasp
or Godzilla flattened cities and spare
characters. Dubbed voices misaligned as the gears
in his brain. Calm always pass-
ing. Childhood tasted like my brother's rage.

My Brother's Collections

It started with the acorns
littering our lawn.
Capped or bald, nibbled or whole—

he wanted them all.
When the wind picked up and Mom
tried to end the collecting, he exploded.

He was still throwing rocks
when my father got home
and forced him into the house.

Things got worse with action
figures (bookcase overturned). Dragons
(phone torn from the wall).

Mostly he wanted monsters—horror movie models
painstakingly glued and painted, then shelved
away from my young, clumsy hands. Stuffed mummies

and King Kongs he'd sometimes share.
Inflatable Frankensteins Dad turned purple
trying to blow up. Swarms of glow-in-the-dark bats.

My brother heaped creatures
on his bed. Slept scrunched to the wall,
surrounded by plastic eyes and felt claws.

Dad patched kicked-in doors
and told me, *Some boys
have a temper.* Cracks

showed through the new paint.
Mom's fingers trembled on the steering
wheel. She scoured malls

to find the final members
of his latest set. He was a bomb
one missing Dracula could detonate.

Heretic

I never got the point of God,
far-away father with his tantrums
and commandments, magic
enough to fix any problem
but usually choosing not to.
Trying to believe, I memorized
the prayers, sang what I was taught,
searched bible stories for things to like—
the ark's zoo of neatly paired animals,
The Red Sea opening like a book.

Job was my last straw.
Not a sinner, not punished,
just tortured so God could
prove something to Satan, a minor
character Jews don't even
give a place to live.

Livelihood gone, children killed,
Job stayed loyal until, pain-dazed,
he asked why, then was
berated for daring to question.
Still, it's taught as a story
that ends happily—more animals,
new kids, his boil-scarred skin soothed,

just like the time I pushed furniture
against my bedroom door,
my brother in one of his fits,
yelling threats, trying to pick the lock
with a screwdriver, then turning
his rage on my dolls,
and afterwards my parents
buying me new ones as though
that made everything all right.

EMILY VOGEL

A Confession

Somewhere, a child mentioned something
with regard to a philosophical quandary
about the grass. What is the grass?
I might answer that the grass
is something that we can depend on
which does not hurt us.

Knowing this, I have a confession to make.

Once, my daughter was playing
with a toy telephone, and I was
busily typing away
at my computer. Whatever it was
I was doing
seemed a matter of life or death,
perhaps to ensure the finances
and livelihood of my children,
but I am not certain.

At any rate, my daughter
was insistent. All she wanted
in the whole world
was for me to play with her
and her telephone.

Instead, in a fit of frustration,
I took her telephone
and threw it.

And in an instant, I was sorry.
I felt like an offensive god, condemning
a child for something
she loved
as much as the feeling
of throbbing inside of my womb.

Her face began to tremble
like a winter moon. The tears
that she so rapidly shed
seemed buoyant, seemed to bounce
from her cheeks,
defiant of any scientific law,
the same way a sun shower in April
seems sometimes
to bounce off the pavement,
makes us somehow consider
that something so sad as rain
is really quite usual.

I am ashamed to tell you this.

Every evening, I make my daughter
a peanut butter sandwich,
and seal it in a bag for school the next day.
I pack her lunch and her school bag,
set her clothes out for the morning,
assiduously. All in all,
she seems quite happy.
But occasionally
I wonder if I am the cause
of some deep sadness
that she harbors
somewhere in the midnight river of her heart,
and if every day of her life
she is grinning wildly, and giggling,
and playing as children do
in spite of it, if that memory
might remain beneath it,
like some resonant phantom,
the dark room in which she sleeps
after I kiss her goodnight
not like any sort of grass at all.

Sad Trees

I cannot tell you enough
just how sad the trees appear
from outside my daughter's window.

People will say, "her mother shut the door
to her room, and lay on the bed,
and did not emerge
for years." They will say
"her mother's spirit
was tethered to the melancholy trees,
and she never wept, but stared,
zombie-eyed, out the evening window."

And I cannot find
many of my daughter's puzzle pieces.
I cannot find the dog, the fish, the frog,
the gerbil. I suppose if I was
a totally ridiculous mom,
I would upheave the entire house
until I found this elusive menagerie.
But I haven't the energy of
well-oiled machines, and my brain
floats and bobs like scum on a pond
in an unbearably warm September.

I go to the window, cannot reconcile myself
to the trees. All of me feels like an absence,
and yet intolerably present
to the pull of juvenile hands, to a scientific
rule, to the madness of infinite starlight.

Gabriel's World

You sit in the middle of the floor
and try to swallow the world,
in the midst of strewn toys, a trailing of stars,
small footprints indented in the carpet,
old crumbs leading to destinations fantastical.
The conundrums of your surroundings
delight you, and you tilt your head
like a planet on its usual orbit—
in an attempt to fathom it,
whatever it is.

Transit

My son has been wont to surges of rage lately.
When dusk finally resigns itself
to the dead-zone of complete dark,
He caterwauls as if something biblical
being slain, runs back and forth and back,
attempts to overturn furniture.
It is as though he's seen the face of God.
Mornings, while he yet still sleeps
like the surface of an August pond,
I drink my coffee, try to settle the debts
of my dreams. I have dreamt of transit,
of being forgotten. For some reason
I think of tulips: how upright they are,
So elegant that they are indifferent.
My son rouses from sleep, seems
to recall nothing of the night prior.
And a white mist seems to effloresce
over this January morning
like anyone's winter ghost.

Circling

A gray scrim falls gently
on the world
at the threshold of dusk.
My daughter holds tight
to my thigh, and repeats
"cows and horses, cows
and horses. Umbrella, rainbow.
I see things in the night."
Then, she gazes
out of the picture window
and says, "I fear moonbeams."
My children are a blazing of sun,
and in some contexts,
I could be the earth, circling them,
mad as the firmament itself.
A singular lamp
glows in a warm room,
as an anonymous moon
also circles me, madly,
and I can feel it
like a whisper, haunting
everything that I am.
All of me, at least for now,
is the night that claims itself,
and does not know
its own sinking.

Mourning Dove

This morning my daughter Clare
clung and wouldn't let go
her legs wrapped around my waist
and her arms pressed to my neck.
I didn't mind wearing her.
If I could wear Clare the rest of my life
well, then so be it.
But we heard the bus up the hill
then saw it riding down: all yellow
and black, putting forth its jazz hands
like some giant black-eyed Susan
into which my little bee climbed
and was gone, the doors closing
behind her, leaving me bare foot
against cold walk and colder lawn.
The silence after she'd been swallowed
was filled with the warmth of her
freshly pulled from me—still leaving
its impress, like a hat you continue to
wear long after it's been fully doffed.
That's when I heard them—the mourning
doves, three perched on the telephone
wires. Are they telephone wires?
One still sleeping with its tiny head
dropped into its chest, but the others
cooed their sad lament, as if to say
there is no end to coming and going and
either becomes the same, after you've
been coming and going long enough
to start to feel the death in things—
not of, but in, and all the coming
is going and all the going is coming
and the bus is a big Black Eyed Susan
and the nape of your daughter's neck
escapes a final kiss as she mounts

the stairs, encouraged by the aid.
Good bye! And hiss of the hydraulic
doors, and then you're here alone
feet numb, listening to the Mourning doves,
those subdued and well-dressed
pigeons, hunted in other parts of the country
to the tune of up to 70 million birds,
So in demand that ideal seed—their
favorite—is planted for the slaughter.
And you wonder what's been planted for your
five-year-old daughter? Who waits at the
top of the stairs and at the end?
At two she began imitating the Mourning doves
that cooed outside her bedroom window
at dawn and dusk. Took you awhile to know
she was learning their song. She mimics
the Mourning dove and the jay. They were
the first birds in her cradle song.
And now the house is empty. There's a dead
Chipmunk left by your cat to let you know
he offer's his share to the larder.
The cat is better now at killing—no marks,
the chipmunk's beautiful. The song
of the Mourning Dove is inside you—
the press of your daughter still against your
chest. You almost coo. Instead you
turn the chipmunk with a hoe, toss him
into the shrubbery. They can dig thirty foot
burrows under your house, destroy the
foundation. Good for them!
The Mourning Dove is not a
peaceful bird. Peace is a construct
it has come to symbolize. It's fierce at
bird feeders, a bully to Sparrows
When the dove drinks it does not lift its
head, but sucks the water in like nectar, sips
its own reflection. When it flees the scene
it makes a high tea kettle whistle
with its wings—a quick flying bird.

My Clare swallows deep and makes the
grieving sound—the gulping coo she's
heard all of her life. She is "non-verbal".
"on the spectrum." Sometimes she clings
so fiercely, at others she pushes me away.
She likes to drum with her hands on my head
It hurts. The dove on over cast days, in
a light rain, appears to be the color of rain—
not so much transparent or translucent, as
the subtlest, leeched pussy willow grey.
My daughter too is sometimes on the verge
of disappearing—rain child with a rain dove coo:
a grey I wear in the bright yellow, the black eyed
Susan of my life. This grief I can bear.
Because a long time ago I learned love does
not refuse the weight that plants it
deep, the weight of the snow on
rods of Forsythia, that causes the rods to bloom,
the weight of my daughter so tight against
my chest, and above me, the doves
crying, heard throughout the land.

Acknowledgements

Special thanks to Sue Elmslie, Oliver de la Paz, Connie Post, Sherine Gilmour, and Tony Gloeggler for your extra help in getting the word out and your support of this project from day one. Big thanks to Sue for putting me in touch with the work of other Canadian writers, and to my old colleague Rumena Buzarovska for putting me in touch with our Israeli contributors.

Gratitude to my wife Lisa M. Dougherty whose own poems were the spark that caused me to examine a broad range of writing on autism and start this project.

And finally gratitude to Amara Rumi, our difficult and exuberant daughter, for her grace and endless grievances, how far you have grown and learned to love and live, despite the odds and evidence. This book is for you.

Meredith Bergmann: "The Ransom" *A Special Education,* 2014; "Nursery Rhyme" *A Special Education,* 2014, *Mezzo Cammin,* 2014, *Women's Voices for Change,* 2015; "Tautavel Man": *A Special Education,* 2014; "Lesson" *A Special Education,* 2014, *Life and Legends* 2015.

Yvonne Blomer: "Pelagic Cormorant" first appeared in *Elegies for Earth,* Leaf Press Overleaf Chapbook, 2018.

Edward Byrne: "Seeking Inklings in an Old Video" appeared in *Tidal Air* by Edward Byrne (Pecan Grove Press, 2002).

Lauren Camp: "Adult Basic Education" was first published in *Amygdala;* "The Dam of Asperger's" in *Little Patuxent Review;* "Traveling with the Ferryman" in *Tinderbox Poetry Journal.*

Barbara Crooker: "Pushing the Stone," "The Children of the Challenger League Enter Heaven," "Washing Diapers," and "Grating Parmesan" appeared in *Barbara Crooker: Selected Poems* (FutureCycle Press, 2015). "Autism Poem: The Grid" appeared in Radiance (Word Press, 2005), "Simile" appeared in *Line Dance* (Word Press, 2008); and "One Word" appeared in *More* (C&R Press, 2010).

Lisa M. Dougherty: "Autism on Earth's Delicate Carpet" appeared in the chapbook *Small as Hope in the Helicopter Rain* (Cervena Barva Books, 2018); "Alongside" first appeared in *Nixes Mate Review.*

Cheryl Dumesnil: "Moon, Jacket, Yellow, Tree, Violin," "Teaching Luca Mr. Potato Head," and "American Robin" appeared in *In Praise of Falling,* by Cheryl Dumesnil, University of Pittsburgh Press, 2009. "Vocabulary" appeared in *Showtime at the Ministry of Lost Causes,* by Cheryl Dumesnil, University of Pittsburgh Press, 2016.

Vivian Eden: "Form and Grace" appeared in *Front and Back* by Vivian Eden, a bilingual volume with translations into Hebrew by various hands, published in 2008 by the Kvar poetry series at the Carmel Press.

Susan Elmslie's poems all were reprinted from *Museum of Kindness* (Brick, 2017).

Rebecca Foust: "Dark Card" first published in *Margie,* "Perfect Target" in *Red Rock Review,* "He Never Lies" in Dark Card, "Eighteen" in *Wordgathering: A Disability Journal,* "Show your Work" and "Homage to Teachers" in *Clackamas Review,* "The Peripheral becomes Crucial" in *Ars Medica,* and all are in *Dark Card* (Texas Review Press, 2008). "An Autist's Mother Reflects" first published in *Mom Egg Review.*

Jennifer Franklin: "Gift," published in *Lips* and *No Small Gift* (Four Way Books, 2018); "Burial of the Brains, Vienna 2002," published at STATOREC and *No Small Gift* (Four Way Books, 2018); "While Waiting *Godot* Interrupts," published in *Prairie Schooner* and *No Small Gift* (Four Way Books, 2018); "Talking to my Daughter After Beckett" first published in *No Small Gift* (Four Way Books, 2018); "My Daughter's Body," published in *Boston Review, Poetry Daily, Borderlands & Crossings: Writing the Motherland* Anthology, Visible Poetry Project film, and *Looming* (Elixir Press, 2015); "I Would Like My Love to Die," published in *Guernica* and *Looming* (Elixir Press, 2015).

Sherine Gilmour: "Injection #3: Compounded Folinic Acid and Subcutaneous Methylcobalamin" appeared in *The Indianapolis Review* (Summer 2017); "Nature" appeared in *The Indianapolis Review*

(Summer 2017); "Sad Animals I" appeared in *The American Journal of Poetry* (January 2017); "Sad Animals II" appeared in *Mom Egg Review* (Volume 15, 2017) and *M.A.M.A.* (Issue 32, July 2018); "Ditches" appeared in *Redivider* (Fall/Winter 2018).

Tony Gloeggler: "Weather" first appeared in *Trajectory* (Fall 2013) and in the chapbook *Tony Come Back August* (2015) "Magnitude" first appeared in *Columbia Poetry Review* (2014) and in *Until The Last Light Leaves* (NYQ Books 2015).

Sonia Greenfield: "Fukushima Daises" previously appeared in *Verse-Virtual,* and "The Lost Boys" appeared in *Boy With a Halo at The Farmer's Market,* Codhill Press, 2015

Max Heinegg: "Advisory" appeared in *Fourth & Sycamore* in April, 2018.

Quraysh Ali Lansana" "echolalia one," "golden," and "flight" appeared in *Hyperlexia Journal;* "echolalia two," "trek," and "the spectrum" appeared in *reluctant minivan* (chapbook), Living Arts Press, Tulsa, 2015.

Joanne Limburg's poems were all reprinted from *The Autistic Alice* (Bloodaxe Books, 2017). Reprinted with permission of Bloodaxe Books and the author.

Shane McCrae's poems are all reprinted from *Mule* (Cleveland State University Poetry Center 2014). Reprinted with permission of CSU and the author.

Megan Merchant: "Cradling an Empty Cup" was Winner, 2016-2017 COG Literary Awards, Issue 10.

Kamilah Aisha Moon's "Love is a Basic Science," "Achilles Tendon: War at 3PM." "(Middle Sister)," "Memory in the Park," "No Room for Gray," and "Directions" all reprinted from *She Has a Name* (c) 2013 by Kamilah Aisha Moon. Reprinted with permission of Four Way Books. All rights reserved.

Oliver de la Paz: "Autism Spectrum Questionnaire: Abnormal Symbolic or Imaginative Play." New England Review. Vol. 39, No. 1. 2018: 73-76. "Autism Screening Questionnaire: Speech and Language Delay." *Poetry.* July/August 2017: 338-341. "Autism Screening Questionnaire: Social Interaction Difficulties." *Indiana Review.* Issue 39, No. 1. Summer 2017: 88-90.

Joel Dias Porter's "Portrait of the Artist as a Starfish in Coffee" is reprinted from *Poetry,* October 2017, with the author's permission.

Connie Post: "Annual Review," "You Are 23 Years Old," "To a Hero Twelve Miles Away," "Non-Verbal, "Cure," "Charlie a Boy in My Son's Group Home" were published in the chapbook *And When the Sun Drops,* Finishing Line Press, 2012.

Celeste Helene Schantz: "The Disappointed Women" first appeared in *Lake Affect Magazine,* Vol. 49 Fall 2016.

Angeline Schellenberg's poems are taken from *Tell Them It Was Mozart* (Brick Books, 2016). "What Happened after He Colored Outside the Line" first appeared in *Rhubarb* magazine (summer 2016).

Alison Stone: "My Brother's Collections" appeared in *Ordinary Magic* (NYQ Books, 2016). "Asperger's" appeared in *Dazzle* (Jacar Press, 2017) "Heretic" appeared in *Caught in the Myth* (NYQ Books, 2019).

Contributor Notes

MEREDITH BERGMANN is a sculptor and poet. Her poems have been published in many journals, including *Barrow Street, Hopkins Review, Hudson Review, Light, Mezzo Cammin, The New Criterion, Raintown Review,* and the anthology *Hot Sonnets.* She was poetry editor of *American Arts Quarterly* from 2006-2017. Her chapbook *A Special Education* was published in 2014 by EXOT Books. Meredith and her husband Michael, a writer and director, live in Connecticut. Their only child, Daniel, lost the ability to speak and was diagnosed with an autism spectrum disorder at age 3. He learned to think and communicate by spelling at age 12, and discovered literature a few weeks later. He's 23 now, and Meredith and Michael drive him to Boston every week so he can study comparative literature and philosophy at Harvard.

YVONNE BLOMER served as the city of Victoria, BC's Poet Laureate from 2015–2018. Her most recent books are *Sugar Ride: Cycling from Hanoi to Kuala Lumpur* (Palimpsest Press, 2017) and *As if a Raven* (Palimpsest, 2014). *Refugium: Poems for the Pacific* (editor, Caitlin Press, 2017) is the first in a trilogy of water-focused environmental poetry anthologies Yvonne is editing. Yvonne's son was born with a rare genetic condition called Prader-Willi Syndrome and at age four was diagnosed with Autism Spectrum Disorder. He is relatively non-verbal but highly communicative. Though she may often ponder the characteristics of each of these conditions and how they shape her son, she also tries to let the boy be the boy he is with all his humour and delight with the world and its own unfathomable quirks.

MATTHEW BORCZON is a nurse and Navy sailor who served in the busiest combat hospital in Afghanistan in 2010-11. It was at this time that his youngest son was diagnosed with a condition on the Autism spectrum. Borczon has been trying to learn more and grow more with his son every day since. He is the author of 8 books of poetry and has been nominated for both a Pushcart Prize and a Best of the Net. His latest book *Ghost Highway Blues* will be out in early 2019 from Alien Buddha Press. Borczon is married with 4 children.

KIM BRIDGFORD writes, "I am the director of Poetry by the Sea and the editor of *Mezzo Cammin*. The author of ten books, I have received grants from the NEA, the Connecticut Commission on the Arts, and the Ucross Foundation. With Russell Goings, I rang the closing bell of the New York Stock Exchange in celebration of his book *The Children of Children Keep Coming*, for which I wrote the introduction. I have been called 'America's First Lady of Form.' I am connected to autism through my sister Kari's son, Sam. His crown made me think of my own relationship to crowns, metrical and otherwise."

EDWARD BYRNE is the author of eight collections of poetry and has edited two anthologies. Much of his work focuses on challenges faced by his family and personal achievements experienced by his son Alex, who is autistic. Byrne's poems have appeared widely in literary journals and his literary criticism has been published in various collections. He is a professor in the English Department at Valparaiso University, where he edits *Valparaiso Poetry Review*.

LAUREN CAMP is the author of four books, including *One Hundred Hungers* (Tupelo Press), finalist for the Arab American Book Award and winner of the Dorset Prize, and Turquoise Door. Her poems have appeared in *The Compass, Ecotone, Beloit Poetry Journal,* and the *Poem-a-Day* series from The Academy of American Poets. A Black Earth Institute Fellow and a 2018 Poet-in-Residence at the Mayo Clinic, she lives and teaches in New Mexico.

BARBARA CROOKER is a poetry editor for *Italian-Americana,* and author of eight full-length books and twelve chapbooks of poetry. Her awards include the WB Yeats Society of New York Award, the Thomas Merton Poetry of the Sacred Award, three Pennsylvania Council on the Arts Creative Writing Fellowships. Her work appears in a variety of literary journals and anthologies, including *The Chariton Poetry Review, Green Mountains Review, Tar River Poetry Review, The Beloit Poetry Journal, The Hollins Critic, Poetry International, The Denver Quarterly, Smartish Pace, Gargoyle, Christianity and Literature, Poetry East, The American Poetry Journal, Dogwood, Zone 3, Passages North, Nimrod, Common Wealth: Contemporary Poets on Pennsylvania, The Bedford Introduction to Literature, Nasty Women: An Unapologetic Anthology of Subversive Verse.* Her work has been read on *The Writer's Almanac* and featured on Ted Kooser's *American Life in Poetry*, and she is the mother of a 34-year-old son with autism.

LISA M. DOUGHERTY is the author of the chapbook *Small as Hope in the Helicopter Rain*, published by Cervena Barva Press, and has published poems in *Congeries, Lake Effect, Nixes Mate, Redactions,* and in the anthology *Double Kiss: Stories, Poems, Essays on the Art of Billiards* (Mammoth Books, 2017). She did not set out to directly write about autism, but rather let the intrigue of her diagnosed daughter shine through what perceptions were previously held normal. In Erie, PA, she navigates with her partner Sean Thomas Dougherty, and their daughters Amara Rumi and Andaluzja Akhmatova.

SEAN THOMAS DOUGHERTY is the author or editor of 16 books including *The Second O of Sorrow*, published by BOA Editions. His awards include a Fulbright Lectureship and two Pennsylvania Council for the Arts Fellowships. He works as a Med Tech and Caregiver for various disabled populations. He lives with the poet Lisa M. Dougherty and their two daughters in Erie, PA. He says, "my poem tries to capture some of the movement of my youngest daughter who was developmentally delayed in so many areas, and yet so simply insightful and verbally imaginative about the world."

CHERYL DUMESNIL'S books include two collection of poems, *Showtime at the Ministry of Lost Causes* and *In Praise of Falling* (winner of the Agnes Lynch Starrett Prize and the Golden Crown Literary Society Prize for Poetry); a memoir, *Love Song for Baby X: How I Stayed (Almost) Sane on the Rocky Road to Parenthood*; and the anthology *Dorothy Parker's Elbow: Tattoos on Writers, Writers on Tattoos*, co-edited with Kim Addonizio. She has taught and learned from children with ASD in creative writing classes and therapeutic settings. She lives in the San Francisco Bay Area with her two sons and her wife, Sarah.

SUSAN ELMSLIE writes "My son was finally diagnosed with autism when he was eight years old, though to us, to many of his educators, and to some other moms of children with autism, it was clear from early on that he was on the spectrum. My poetry collection, *Museum of Kindness* (Brick, 2017)—longlisted for the Pat Lowther Memorial Award—devotes a section to my experience of parenting in a family when a child has special needs. My first collection, *I, Nadja, and Other Poems* (Brick, 2006), won the A.M. Klein Poetry Prize and was shortlisted for the McAuslan First Book Prize, the Pat Lowther, and a ReLit Award. My poems have also appeared in the *Best Canadian Poetry in English* (2008, 2015), and the *Best of the Best Canadian Poetry* (2017). I've been a Hawthornden Poetry Fellow. Since 2003, I've taught English and Creative Writing at Dawson College in Montreal."

VIVIAN EDEN holds a doctorate in comparative literature from the University of Iowa and has taught English, theater and translation in various academic and informal settings. Currently she is on the staff of *Haaretz English Edition*, a newspaper associated with the International New York Times. She was born in the United States, lives in Jerusalem and is the mother of two beloved children, one of whom has autism and the other of whom is his younger sister and is devoted to him.

REBECCA FOUST'S books include *Paradise Drive*, winner of the 2015 Press 53 Award for Poetry and reviewed in venues including the *Times Literary Supplement*. Recent recognitions include the Cavafy Prize, the James Hearst Poetry Prize, the Lascaux Flash Fiction Prize, the *American Literary Review* Fiction Prize, the Constance Rooke Creative Nonfiction Prize, and fellowships from Hedgebrook, MacDowell, Sewanee, The Frost Place, and West Chester Poetry Conference. Foust is the mother of an adult son on the spectrum and received a California Golden Bell award in 2008 for her work in autism advocacy in the schools. She was the 2017-19 Poet Laureate of Marin County and is the Poetry Editor for *Women's Voices for Change*, writing a weekly column since 2015.

JENNIFER FRANKLIN (AB Brown University, MFA Columbia University School of the Arts) is the author of *No Small Gift* (Four Way Books 2018) and *Looming* (Elixir 2015). Her poetry has appeared widely in anthologies, literary magazines, and journals including *Blackbird, Gettysburg Review, Paris Review*, "poem-a-day" on *poets.org, Poetry Daily, Prairie Schooner*, and *Verse Daily*. A selection of her poetry is featured in the autism chapter of Andrew Solomon's National Book Critics Circle award-winning book, *Far from the Tree* (Scribner 2012). She is co-editor of Slapering Hol Press and teaches poetry manuscript compilation and revision at the Hudson Valley Writers' Center, where she serves as Program Director. She raised her eighteen-year old daughter (with profound autism and epilepsy) alone. They live in New York City with the rescue pitbull therapy dog who changed their lives.

SHERINE GILMOUR began writing about autism after her son was diagnosed. The experience of the diagnostic process and meeting many other parents through her son's early intervention program inspired much of this work. She has been nominated for a Pushcart Prize, and her poems have appeared in *American Journal of Poetry, Mom Egg Review, Redivider, So To Speak, SWWIM, Tinderbox,* and other publications.

TONY GLOEGGER writes "I live in NYC and I started working in a group home for the developmentally disabled in 1979 and have been managing it for 35 years. But my real connection to autism is through the son of an ex-girlfriend. We reconnected in around 2000 and her son Jesse was five at the time and severely autistic. Immediately I was drawn to him and when we decided to move in together I took him in and treated him as if he was my son. Things didn't work out with me and his mom, but I still feel as if Jesse is just a little bit mine and I do all I can for him. He lives in Maine and I spend 8 or 9 weekends a year and just being around him makes me feel better about everything. I am happy to say that he is a happy 24-year-old guy who lives in his own apartment. He has a full and happy life thanks to his mom's incredible love, hard headed advocacy and the brilliant foresight to create a unique model that works for Jesse." My book *Until The Last Light Leaves* focuses on my group home job and my continuing connection to Jesse (NYQ Books, 2015).

ADAM GRABOWSKI'S poetry has appeared in *DMQ Review, jubilat, Beech St. Review,* and elsewhere. He has a poem in the forthcoming anthology *What Saves Us: Poems of Empathy and Rage in the Age of Trump,* edited by Martín Espada. Adam has been fighting with various public school officials for years, ever since his oldest child was diagnosed with autism at the age of four. His poem in this anthology speaks to those years. Adam received his MSW from Westfield State University in 2012 and is currently an MFA candidate at the Vermont College of Fine Arts. A regional representative for masspoetry.org, he teaches poetry at the Pioneer Valley Writers' Workshop and lives in Holyoke, Ma with his wife and two children.

Sonia Greenfield was born and raised in Peekskill, New York, and her chapbook, *American Parable*, won the 2017 Autumn House Press/Coal Hill Review prize. Her first full-length collection, *Boy with a Halo at the Farmer's Market*, won the 2014 Codhill Poetry Prize. Her work has appeared in the *2018* and *2010 Best American Poetry, Antioch Review, Bellevue Literary Review, Los Angeles Review, Massachusetts Review,* and *Willow Springs,* among others. Her collection of prose poems, *Letdown*, is forthcoming in 2020 with White Pine Press as part of the Marie Alexander Series. She lives with her family in Hollywood, California where she advocates for her autistic son, edits the *Rise Up Review*, and directs the Southern California Poetry Festival.

George Guida has published seven books, including *The Pope Stories and Other Tales of Troubled Times* (2012) and four collections of poems, most recently *Pugilistic* (2015) and *The Sleeping Gulf* (2015). In 2006 George visited a Bolivian orphanage, where he saw autistic and cognitively challenged children tethered to window bars and otherwise neglected by an overwhelmed staff.

Max Heinegg is an English teacher who lives in Medford, MA, where he has taught in the public schools for 21 years. His poems have appeared in *The Cortland Review, Columbia Poetry Review,* and *The American Journal of Poetry*, among others. In his time in the classroom, he's seen autism go from a mystery that was often unexplored, to something that every teacher needs to understand and prepare for, especially English teachers. Working with students with autism on a daily basis has deepened his understanding of the role language plays in communication, and of the profound impact that attention and positivity has in the life of all students.

Quraysh Ali Lansana is author of eight poetry books, three textbooks, three children's books, editor of eight anthologies, and coauthor of a book of pedagogy. He is a Humanities Teacher at Holland Hall School, and is a former faculty member of the Writing Program of the School of the Art Institute of Chicago and the Drama Division of The Juilliard School. Lansana served as Director of the Gwendolyn Brooks Center for Black Literature and Creative Writing at Chicago State University from 2002-2011, where he was also Associate Professor of English/Creative Writing until 2014.

Recent books include *The Whiskey of Our Discontent: Gwendolyn Brooks as Conscience & Change* Agent (Haymarket Books, 2017); Revise *the Psalm: Work Celebrating the Writings of Gwendolyn Brooks* (Curbside Splendor, 2017); *A Gift from Greensboro (Penny Candy Books, 2016); The BreakBeat Poets: New American Poetry in the Age of Hip Hop* (Haymarket Books, 2015).

JOANNE LIMBURG is a British writer, poet and creative writing lecturer, who was diagnosed with autism in 2012, at the age of 42. She wrote the sequence *The Autistic Alice* as a way of retrieving her lost autistic childhood and girlhood. Her publications include three poetry collections; the novel *A Want of Kindness*, published in the US by Pegasus books; memoirs *The Woman Who Thought Too Much* and *Small Pieces*. She lives in Cambridge, England with her husband and son, and teaches creative writing at De Montfort University in Leicester.

AYALA BEN LULU is an Israeli poet and writer. She holds degrees in psychology and the history of ideas. Her debut book *Shortened Childhood* (Pardes Publishing House 2013) won a number of literary awards, including the Culture Minister's Prize. Her second book, *Taste of Daughter* (Afik publishing house) was published in 2016. Ayala has a child with autism for whom she manages a unique therapy program.

SHANE MCCRAE writes, "I wrote these poems in response to my son's autism diagnosis. At the time during which I was writing them, I often felt the diagnosis sitting beside my son, asking for a kind of attention I didn't know how to give, an attention separate from the attention I gave him. The poems arose, as my poems often do, unbidden though wished-for—in this particular instance, in response to questions I found myself asking about my son's diagnosis. The only kinds of questions I can answer with poems are questions for which I do not have answers. The poems arose from my bewilderment. Currently, I live in New York City, and teach at Columbia University. I have published six full-length collections of poetry, most recently *The Gilded Auction Block*. I have received a Lannan Literary Award, a Whiting Writer's Award, an Anisfield-Wolf Book Award, and a fellowship from the NEA."

MEGAN MERCHANT lives in the tall pines of Prescott, AZ with her husband and two children. She is the author of three full-length poetry collections with Glass Lyre Press: *Gravel Ghosts* (2016), *The Dark's Humming* (2015 Lyrebird Award Winner, 2017), *Grief Flowers* (2018), four chapbooks, and a children's book, *These Words I Shaped for You* (Philomel Books). She was awarded the 2016-2017 COG Literary Award, judged by Juan Felipe Herrera, the 2018 Beullah Rose Poetry Prize, and most recently, second place in the Pablo Neruda Prize for Poetry. She is an Editor at *The Comstock Review*.

KAMILAH AISHA MOON is a Pushcart Prize winner, CLMP Firecracker Award and Lambda Award finalist, and a 2015 New American Poet who has received fellowships to Vermont Studio Center, Rose O'Neill Literary House, Hedgebrook, and Cave Canem. The author of *Starshine & Clay* (2017) and *She Has a Name* (2013), both published by Four Way Books, her work has been featured widely, including the *Harvard Review, Poem A Day, Boston Review, Prairie Schooner* and elsewhere. Moon holds an MFA from Sarah Lawrence College and is an Assistant Professor of Poetry and Creative Writing at Agnes Scott College in Decatur, Georgia.

OLIVER DE LA PAZ is the author of five books of poetry, most recently *Post Subject: A Fable* with a forthcoming fifth entitled *The Boy in the Labyrinth*. He is the father of three sons on the Autism Spectrum and happily balances family life with his job teaching students at the College of the Holy Cross and in the Low Res MFA Program at Pacific Lutheran University.

JOEL DIAS PORTER (aka DJ Renegade) was born and raised in Pittsburgh, PA, and lives with Asperger's Syndrome. From 1994-1999 he competed in the National Poetry Slam, and was the 1998 and 99 Haiku Slam Champion. His poems have been published in; *Time Magazine, The Washington Post, Best American Poetry 2014, Mead, POETRY, Callaloo, Ploughshares, Antioch Review, Red Brick Review, Asheville Review, Beltway Quarterly* and the anthologies *Gathering Ground, Love Poetry Out Loud, Meow: Spoken Word from the Black Cat, Short Fuse, Role Call, Def Poetry Jam, 360 Degrees of Black Poetry, Slam (The Book), Revival: Spoken Word from Lollapallooza, Poetry Nation, Beyond the Frontier, Spoken Word Revolution, Catch a Fire,* and *The Black Rooster*

Social Inn. In 1995, He received the Furious Flower "Emerging Poet Award." Performances include the Today Show, SlamNation, on BET, and the film Slam. A Cave Canem fellow, he has a CD of jazz and poetry entitled 'LibationSong'.

CONNIE POST served as Poet Laureate of Livermore, California (2005 to 2009). Her work has appeared in many journals including *Calyx, Comstock Review, Cold Mountain Review, Slipstream, River Styx, Atticus Review, Spoon River Poetry Review, Valparaiso Poetry Review, Glint,* and *Verse Daily.* Her first full-length book, *Floodwater* (Glass Lyre Press 2014), won the Lyrebird Award. Her chapbook, *And When the Sun Drops,* is about her adult son with profound autism. It won the Aurorean Fall 2012 Editor's Choice award. Her poetry awards include the 2018 Pirene's Fountain Liakoura Award, the 2016 Crab Creek Poetry Award and the Caesura Poetry Award. Connie has been an advocate for autism since the early 1990's. She helps parents with challenges during diagnosis and education. She has served as the keynote speaker at special needs conferences and has given many presentations at colleges. Her poems about autism appear in many nonfiction books about autism.

CELESTE SCHANTZ is the runner-up for the Stephen Dunn Poetry Prize, judged by Terrance Hayes. Her poems appear in *Solstice, Fugue, Stone Canoe,* and other journals. Her first essay, on postpartum depression, is forthcoming in *Fugue's* Spring 2019 issue. Schantz works for the public library. She's raising her son in Upstate New York, where she champions his Autism, Tourette Syndrome, and other issues. She's currently working on her first book of poems.

ANGELINE SCHELLENBERG is the mother of two teenagers on the autism spectrum, with whom she shares a love for *Star Wars.* Her first book *Tell Them It Was Mozart* (Brick Books, 2016)—linked poems about motherhood—won the Lansdowne Prize for Poetry, the Eileen McTavish Sykes Award for Best First Book, the John Hirsch Award for Most Promising Manitoba Writer, and was a finalist for the 2017 ReLit Award for poetry. Her work has appeared in numerous journals, including *The New Quarterly, Prairie Fire, Grain, Wordgathering,* and *Lemon Hound,* and in her chapbook *Roads of Stone* (Alfred Gustav Press,

2015). Her chapbook *Dented Tubas* is forthcoming with Kalamalka Press in May 2019. Angeline lives in Winnipeg, Canada.

ALISON STONE has published six collections, *Caught in the Myth* (NYQ Books, 2019), *Dazzle* (Jacar Press, 2017), *Masterplan*, collaborative poems with Eric Greinke (Presa Press, 2018), *Ordinary Magic* (NYQ Books, 2016), *Dangerous Enough* (Presa Press, 2014), and *They Sing at Midnight*, which won the 2003 Many Mountains Moving Poetry Award; as well as three chapbooks. Her poems have appeared in *The Paris Review, Poetry, Ploughshares, Poet Lore,* and many others. She has been awarded *Poetry*'s Frederick Bock Prize and *New York Quarterly*'s Madeline Sadin Award. She is also a painter and created The Stone Tarot. During her extensive training as a therapist, she was never taught about autism or the spectrum. (Hopefully this has changed now.) A magazine article finally gave her answers to why her brother was the way he was, and further research helped her to see these neurological patterns in both her father and herself.

EMILY VOGEL'S poetry, translations, reviews, and essays have been published widely, most recently in *Omniverse, The North American Review, Tiferet,* and *PEN*. She is the author of five chapbooks and three full length collections, the most recent being *Dante's Unintended Flight* (NYQ Books 2017). Both of her children are autistic, and much of her poetry derives from her experiences with this. She has a children's book due to be released in the spring of 2019 titled *Clara's Song* (Swingin' Bridge Books) based on her daughter's experiences with her disability and uncanny talent for music. Emily teaches writing at SUNY Oneonta, and is married to the poet, Joe Weil. They live in Binghamton, and their children attend The Institute For Child Development at Binghamton University.

JOE WEIL teaches poetry to graduate and undergraduate students at Binghamton University. He is father to Clare and Gabriel Vogel Weil, both of whom are "on the spectrum." He is married to the poet and children's author, Emily Vogel. His most recent book is *A Night in Duluth* published by NYQ Books in 2016.